Equipment

Additional books by author:

Firehouse Fraternity Oral History Series:
Volume I: Becoming a Firefighter
Volume II: Life Between Alarms
Volume IV: Responding
Volume V: Riots to Renaissance
Volume VI: Changing the NFD

The Newark Riots: A View from the Firehouse

Fiction:
The Firebox Stalker
The Hand Life Dealt you
A-zoe: A Woman in Interesting Times

Children's Fiction
Balancing Act (Middle Grade)
A Hundred Battles (YA)
A Broken Glass (YA)

The Firehouse Fraternity

An Oral History of the
Newark Fire Department

Volume III

Equipment

Neal Stoffers

Springfield and Hunterdon Publishing

www.newarkfireoralhistory.com

First Printing: 2008

ISBN: 978-1-970034-12-7

Springfield and Hunterdon Publishing
East Brunswick, NJ 08816-5852

www.NewarkFireOralHistory.com

Dedicated to past, present, and future generations of Newark firefighters, and especially to the 67 firefighters who made the ultimate sacrifice upholding their oath to protect the lives and property of Newark's citizens.

Contents

Acknowledgements

The credit for much of this book goes to the members of the Newark Fire Department who gave so generously of their time to take part in my oral history project. The hours of recorded conversations they contributed will help preserve the history of Newark's fire department and of Newark itself. A list of those interviewed appears at the end of the book. This is their story. I am honored to tell it.

Foreword

This book is one of six which recount the experiences of Newark firefighters. Beginning with the memories of a firefighter appointed in 1942, they tell the story of New Jersey's largest city and her fire department as seen through the eyes of the men manning her firehouses. I have attempted to group related subjects together to give the reader a true feel for various aspects of the fire service. The comments of the men I interviewed are presented in order of appointment date. This method is an attempt to give a better picture of the chronology of the dramatic changes which occurred in the city of Newark and the fire service in general.

The seeds of these books were unknowingly planted in a small firehouse on Springfield Avenue and Hunterdon Street. It was here as a young firefighter that I sat in the kitchen of Six Engine and listened to conversations between veteran firefighters, captains, and Deputy Chiefs about a city and fire department that existed in another time.

In June of 1991, I began an oral history project to preserve the memories of these men and the generations of firefighters who followed. The purpose of this project was to capture not only the words, but the texture of their experiences. What was a firefighting career like during this period in Newark and by extrapolation in America? Fire departments across the country have shared the experiences of the NFD in one way or another. Whether read by a professional firefighter from New York City or by a volunteer firefighter from a small rural community, the stories will be familiar. The fire service is a small world with a common purpose.

It is hoped what is recorded here will show both a bygone era and the evolution of the Newark Fire Department into its present form. If others outside the fire service walk away with a better understanding of the firefighters and the fire departments that protect them, my time over the past years will have been well spent.

Chapter One: Engines

Fredette: We had the Fox. Nine Engine had two pieces. The hose wagon had solid tires and a forty gallon booster tank. No pumps, but we had two CO_2 extinguishers hooked up to the tank. When we would go to a fire we used to crank the valves and that would create the pressure to this booster tank. We only had forty gallons of water and that booster. When those forty gallons went out, you had better have a two and a half ready. I got to learn to stretch a two and a half up at Nine Engine because you had to stretch two and a half for supply. Forty gallons went pretty fast.

The Ahrens-Fox was the one with the big ball. It had two wheel brakes, no power steering. It was rough. The steering wheel was on the right side and we had the hand brake on the outside of the apparatus. It was hard to stop. We drove through gas stations to avoid having accidents. You couldn't stop the engine, so we went right through gas stations up on Springfield Avenue.

Then we had the soda and acid extinguishers for a while. They took them off because they claimed it did more damage than the fire itself.

Vetrini: We had an Ahrens-Fox with the dome pulsator on the rig in the front and we had a Ford hose wagon. The Ford hose wagon carried the two lays of twenty lengths on each side.

Redden: An American LaFrance, it was like a 1924 version. Chain drive, they had just replaced the solid tires with pneumatic tires. Right hand drive and everything is on the right. The foot brakes didn't work that well. These are the mechanical foot brakes. Then you had a windshield that came up to about your shoulders, a little mica windshield. It was a rotary gear pump, side suction with a churn valve, and a fifty gallon booster tank.

If you hooked up to a hydrant and threw the pumps in immediately, you could stall out everything. The churn valve allowed you to let the water come in uniformly to get the rotary gear pumping and pumping out. You had to operate the churn valve. It wasn't automatic and of course you were shown that. You practiced it. You trained at it. I think essentially when they first started getting motorized pumpers, Ahrens-Fox was number one. That was the oldest one. Then you start getting the rotary gear pumpers in and possibly when I went on the job it might have been half and half. Then by the time I got down to Sixteen Engine, they started buying centrifugal pumpers.

Kinnear: At Six Engine we had an Ahrens-Fox. I guess it was from the '30s probably, maybe early '40s. It had the big ball on the front, the big vacuum chamber that impressed people. Everyone rode on the back step. It probably was a five hundred gallon per minute pumper. There was even one engine that we got as a spare that still had a chain drive. Trucks had wooden ladders. They were eighty to a hundred footers at the time. I remember one chief's car which had a trunk that opened but in the shape of a car with a rumble seat. That was a spare, too.

Masters: These old apparatus were all chain driven. It was quite an experience. When I first walked into the firehouse the engine had an Ahrens-Fox. I think it had a hundred gallon booster tank. That was right behind the driver where the gas tank was. When you shoveled hydrants for the Ahrens-Fox, you had to shovel them out a certain way. Instead of straight, you shoveled at an angle. This way the apparatus could pull right into the hydrant. Some of the old rigs had the four inch connection on the rear of the rig instead of the front. Ours was an old rig, but the suction was

2

in the front. You had to back in with the rear suction. I liked the front hook up better.

F. Grehl: The equipment was basically the same. You had the pumpers, basically thousand gallon pumpers, a few seven hundred fifties in there. They had some specialized equipment. Over the course of the years, the newer apparatus we got were more modern, up to date, more efficient, and basically improved as far as the operation. The basic operations are the same.

We had ten two-piece companies. Each of those two-piece companies was almost equivalent to operating alone except they were smaller pumpers. The early ones, the older ones we had were two hundred and fifty gallon pumpers, but most of them were five hundred gallon a minute. Then later they went to seven hundred and fifty gallon pumpers. When they got seven-fifty, every time we had a break down and we had no spares around they took this extra unit from the two-piece units. It was another one of the reasons for the decline in two-piece units. Why should we buy ten more pumpers? The equipment keeps improving to make for greater efficiency. The apparatus is the same except it's tremendously improved today compared to what it was before.

Six Engine had an old Ahrens-Fox which was from 1927 or '29, somewhere in there. Twenty-nine Engine was in a Jewish community in which the politics was of an important nature. Mayor Olenstien was a Jew and so Twenty-nine got a pretty new apparatus, 1937 or '39 Ward LaFrance. It wasn't until 1948 that they bought all these American LaFrance rigs, which were the cab forward. That was the first new basic modern ones that they were buying, American LaFrance. Before that they had Ward LaFrance and Ahrens-Fox. But then they went pretty exclusively to American LaFrance.

3

In 1953 they bought a whole other bunch of the same type of apparatus. These had a hundred and fifty gallon booster tanks. Also in the '50s, '52 somewhere in there, they started buying Macks. They didn't change the booster tank. It was still a hundred and fifty gallons, so there wasn't much improvement.

One of the reasons there wasn't much improvement in there was there was no basic input from the field. You had the guys who were God down there in headquarters. They didn't listen to anybody else. They did what they wanted and didn't ask the people in the field what to do. It really wasn't until Chief Sommers took over that it changed. He was the one who started going and talking to the Deputy Chiefs and the Battalion Chiefs to find out, "What do you need?"

I was a captain at the time and they asked me, "We're going to get a new apparatus for you, what do you want?" So, I said, "One of the things I want is a thirty-foot three section extension ladder on the rig. We have twenty-fours and they just won't reach. We get there. We're all alone a lot of times. The truck companies are coming, but we're all alone with people hanging. I think you ought to get a thirty-foot and we can reach up there with that. We can do some rescues." Sommers went along with it. Now all apparatus have it. Sommers used to listen to what the people were talking about.

We had no compartments in those days on apparatus. Everything that you had was up on the top. There were boards that covered the hose bed and everything was on top of the boards. When you had a fire and you had to change the hose and everything, you had to take all the stuff off the top. Then take all the boards out, put all the hose back in, and then put all the stuff back on top. So, the fellows didn't like to stretch hose, no less have to change it.

The pumps on the Ahrens-Fox were what they call positive displacement piston type pumps. They got into the centrifugal pumps with those LaFrances when they came. Very confusing because they had to be primed and the old timers were tough, like anybody else. Nobody's going to accept anything new out there. "I've been doing this for fifty years and this is the best way." It took a while to get them acclimated to priming pumps and the tricks of priming it. There was a fellow who was pretty good at it.

We used to go down and take the test on the pumps. When you draft you had an automatic prime with a piston pump. It would just pump the air right out of everything. But with a centrifugal pump you have to prime it. They have oil reservoirs to prime it and they have a little positive displacement pump in there. We used to pull out a leaver to prime it, it would engage that particular little pump, expel the air from there, and expel the air from the suction hose. Afterwards atmospheric pressure would take over and push the water back up. This particular fellow at Eighteen Engine was always the best at pumper priming. We found out that instead of doing all that, he would open the tank valve and let all the water flow down and fill the whole pump up. He had water almost instantly, the little tricks.

When I first went on the job, they had open cabs with windshields that came up to your chest. You sat very, very high on the American LaFrance and the Ward LaFrance at the time. All the wind, the snow, and the bugs would hit you. Sommers was one of the first Chiefs who got the closed cabs. How much is it going to cost to close a cab? How much would it have cost to put heaters in? Well, that was another five or six years before we could get a heater put in the cab because that was an extra fifty or a hundred dollars on the cost.

When the American LaFrance came through in 1948 and 1953 at least the windshields were higher than you. It was still an open cab. Those apparatus and the Macks were basically the same, open cab with higher

5

windshield. They're the ones we had in the riots. We had a lot of them in service. When they were throwing things from the rooftops, they built these plywood covers over to protect the men. And they built the plywood covers over the back step, to protect the men there, too. When they came through with those American LaFrances, we had the little bucket seats. They were the first ones that had bucket seats.

McCormack: The first fire engine that I had in the company was an American LaFrance rotary positive displacement pumper, one thousand gallons per minute. It had all the old stuff on it, the steam port boiler on the side and the Ross relief valve. The pumps were positive displacement, which meant that if you shut down a line too fast, the water hammer would travel all the way back to the engine and if the relief bar wasn't properly set, you might stall the engine. They taught you to open and close the nozzle slowly. It all locked in together, so you had to close the valve slowly down when you were shutting down. In the main, you had to open it slowly when you opened it.

A lot of the rigs had right wheel drives. Most of them had mechanical brakes, no hydraulic brakes. You had to literally stand on the brakes to get them to stop. If you were rolling and you wanted to stop, you grabbed the hand brake, pulled up as hard as you could with one hand and stood on the brakes with your foot. Sometimes you put two feet on the brake and pushed on it because it was a spring actuated mechanical braking system, through levers and everything else, which pulled the brake shoes. There were no hydraulic cylinders in there to multiply your factor. It was strictly muscle power to stop this thing.

For some reason or another, a lot of these rigs were right hand drives. The steering wheel was like the English system, on the opposite side of the rig. I really don't know why that was. None of the cars were that way. None of the trucks were that way. I mean over the road trucks, delivery trucks. The only thing I remember being like that was the fire engines. There must have been a reason for it, but I don't know why.

You pulled the hand brake with your right hand. It was outside of the cab. You grabbed it and pulled it up. The clutch you operated with your left foot and the brake you operated with your right foot conventionally, but you were on the wrong side of the seat when you drove. None of the rigs in those days had closed cabs. That was a no-no. The reason was people felt in the fire service in those days that a closed cab would restrict your vision. With open cabs the officer and the driver were able to see down the street, see what they were getting into; see the fire. If you had a closed cab, you would be restricted because you'd be peering through a windshield.

So until the advent of the '60s when the civil disturbances and everything came in, we had all open cabs. To protect the firefighters from rocks and bottles and things thrown off tall buildings at them, they started constructing plywood shields over the driver's cab, to protect the captain and the driver. After that fire manufacturers started to make outfits that had closed cabs and then it became accepted. Now they're all closed cabs, but I remember if you talked about closed cabs before that time old timers would say, "You can't have a closed cab. Are you crazy? You can't see anything in closed cabs. How are you going to see the fire if you have closed cabs?"

Masterson: They had the two pieces in Ten Engine. They just got a new Mack. It was something, brand new. We were always looking at a really nice piece of equipment. It was one of the first Macks that came out. And they had a Ford hose wagon which never started when the bell hit. The battery was always low.

Deutch: I was assigned to the foam truck, Thirty-five Engine at Newark Airport and the traffic circle. It had eight large cylinders of CO_2 in the back. Then we had the inch and a half with six hundred thirty gallons of water for other fires or flushing down. It was designed by Chief Sommers; strictly for highway fires and to help Newark Airport out in case of small fires. At that time they weren't as big a setup as they are today. We ended up fighting more brush fires than anything because we had a lot of brush around us. And all the stuff down Doremus Avenue, we used to get quite a bit of work down there with it. But Thirty-five wasn't a busy company. The highway was busy, but in those days it just wasn't as busy as it is today.

McGrory: We still had some of the positive displacement pumps in the city, but very few were first line. Most of the engines had centrifugal pumps. A lot of the truck companies still had wooden ladders. The equipment was pretty good, but it was gasoline driven, which can't compare to diesel with the power and everything. There were a lot of differences. We had 1948 and '49 American Frances mostly. They were like bathtubs. They were all open. All the trucks were open. The only closed cab fire apparatus were the hose wagons. The Macks we had were all open.

They were hard to steer, no power brakes, all manual transmissions, and the soft suctions were on the rear of some of these rigs. Taking the hydrant was a job; most of the time you took it by yourself. If you took it wrong, you'd block the street; then you'd get hell. It's very easy to block

8

the street. It's easy with the front-end hook ups to take a hydrant. But you had visibility with the open rigs. Quite a few of them were underpowered. They'd scream about old Nine Truck trying to get up Avon Avenue hill. Luckily most of their runs were downhill. They weren't powered the way they should have been. The rigs today are a lot better.

There was no compartment space. On the American LaFrances there were a couple of little compartments on the side and one in the very rear. Most of your stuff was kept up by the hose reel or on top of the boards. You had the fenders coming over the rear wheels and then you had the extinguishers and your strainer for you hard suction on the back step. You were very limited in space, but the big thing was the capacity of your booster tank. Booster tank is a misnomer really, but that's what it was a booster tank. Three hundred gallons was the norm for quite a while. You could do a lot. I don't know exactly when five hundred gallon tanks came in. There were a lot of three hundreds. They went from one hundred gallons to maybe two hundred in some of the wagons to three hundred. It hasn't been too many years that it's five hundred. They had a problem with the tanks because they started rusting out. You'd have all kinds of problems. We used to leak a lot of water.

In the old American LaFrances we didn't have a positive pressure priming system. It was done off the Venturi valve. The Venturi valve was nothing but the air escaping, going across an opening, making a partial vacuum in the pump, and therefore the water being able to push up into your pump. We had a lot of problems with leaking pumps. Guys used to start the engines when they came in to make sure they had prime. A lot of times you didn't because of leaking pumps. You'd lose prime. It got so bad that a mechanic put a petcock on top of the pumps that we used to open because

9

the top of the tank, your booster tank, was higher than your pump. You'd open the booster tank to the pump, open the petcock, and it'd fill the pump up. After that you didn't have to start the engine to see if you had prime. We used to come in with the old American LaFrances, open your tank to pump, then open that petcock and she'd fill up. You'd have prime for a while anyway.

Another thing with those American LaFrances, you might have them in the wrong gear. You used to have to engage it manually. It's changed dramatically with the rigs, a pretty big change over the time since I first came on. But it's been progressive. It hasn't been one bang.

Charpentier: We had the John Bean with the high-pressure pump in Six Engine. When used properly it was really a good piece of equipment. You had seven hundred and fifty pounds of pressure at the nozzle. You could put your hand in front of the nozzle when it was on fog and the stream would be as smooth as felt. You put it on straight stream and you could wash wallpaper off the walls or take the mortar out from between the bricks. But most of the apparatus were either Macks or American LaFrances. Most of the Macks were new ones. They were in pretty good shape. The guys took pride in maintaining their equipment. Whether it was a slow company or a busy company, you had your work to do on your schedule and you did it.

Freda: I couldn't wait to drive this big red fire engine around until I found a spare in the house that had a magneto on it. This thing was antique. The fire department had a spare in that bay that had a magneto on it. A magneto is a device with two levers that sit underneath the steering wheel. You had to set it by sliding them back and forth. It set the spark. That was the ignition. The siren was a chain coming into the cab on the captain's side

10

that was hooked up to the flywheel and you pulled on it. The siren went up. It hit the flywheel and spun. That's what made the siren noise. The motor was so loud that you couldn't hear the siren because they didn't have mufflers on the rigs then. They could hear it coming without the siren. You could hear this thing coming a block or two away.

Smith: Well, the rigs were open cab. We had a second piece, a hose wagon, that was a closed cab and we had a Mack with an open cab. They were all manual transmissions. There were no automatic transmissions.

Dunn: We had a lot of two-piece engine companies at one time with a hose wagon and a pumper. For whatever reason, separate sections of the city ran these units differently. We used the two-piece engine company specifically in the East Ward because of the long hose lays necessitated by our industrial areas. We had a lot more industrial type of fires. We didn't have too much private fire protection in the companies. When we did have a fire off Doremus Avenue or a major industrial area, we would need a lot of hose to get that first line in operation. That has been phased out over the period of the last twenty-five years.

Carragher: Nine Engine had a 1948 American LaFrance. Right after World War II, Civil Defense funds came into the city. They got apparatus in 1946, '47, and '48 through the Federal government. They had an American LaFrance thousand-gallon pumper with an open cab. It was a windshield, nothing else. We also had a brand new International hose wagon with a three hundred gallon tank. That's one of the ones that had that hydraulic deck pipe on it. You could stand on the back step and operate your deck

11

pipe from the ground with the water pressure going in. It controlled it. You could move it around and up and down, which was a nice feature.

The rest of the rigs were very similar. Twenty-eight had an American LaFrance. Fifteen had an American LaFrance. Fifteen had an old hose wagon. I think it was a Ford. They had gas engines and standard transmissions. Double clutching to shift and no power steering, but the old Ahrens-Fox with the steering wheel on the right, hand brake, and mechanical brakes were all gone when I came on.

When I went to the Rescue Squad, they had that Guttenberg. It was a Ford chassis, Ford cab and it had the modernized back on it. You could sit up inside it, very similar to the rescue today. A little different shape, but it was very similar to the Squad today. It was an enclosed rig. We used to transport victims in that too at the time because then they didn't mind you transporting. I remember going to a three-alarm fire on Orange Street in that rig. Doctor Devlin used to ride with the Rescue Squad all the time. We were coming back and we all had headaches. He started to get a headache. He said, "Hey, I'm getting a headache. Something is wrong." We come back to the firehouse and we check the rig and the exhaust pipe is bad. All the exhaust is coming right up into the cab where we were all sitting, right there, carbon monoxide poisoning for us all.

Twenty Engine had a Mack. I think a '52 Mack and they had an International hose wagon also with a five hundred gallon tank. The first five hundred gallon tank in the city I think was Twenty Engine with the hose wagon. It was an International. The International had power steering. The Mack didn't. The Mack had manual steering, so when you made a turn on that you were fighting that wheel all the way. But everything else was hydraulic on it. Then I went to Six Engine and they got the Ward LaFrance diesel right after the riots in '67.

Haran: In Salvage they actually called the rig a horse wagon. That's what it looked like. It was a Ford with a two-seater cab. It had all cabinets on the side, but it didn't look like what they call a bread truck today. It had a canopy over half the back and half the back was enclosed. They had doors going in to get you out of the weather. But when it was nice, you could sit outside responding to a fire. They were basically the same look as the old Rescue Squad and had a separate cab. Of course they were old looking back then. Today all our apparatus are maybe four years old.

In 1961 they had old, open-cab American LaFrances. Some of them were 1947 and the early '50s. I'm talking in 1961, '62. A lot of our apparatus were fifteen, eighteen, twenty years old back then. We had a lot of Macks. They got away from Macks because they were too expensive. Everything today is E-Ones.

Cahill: We had mostly Macks and American LaFrances. The American LaFrances were probably the older. Macks were the replacements. Of course, a lot of the companies got the hand me downs. It's still happening today. In Five Engine we'd get a Mack hand me down from somebody up in the First Division. They would get the new one. That hasn't changed. The Macks were great. They had tremendous energy. You couldn't screw it up. It was just pump to pump to pump to pump. It wasn't so much that they were kept up. It was just great equipment. The cabs were open until, I guess, the riots.

Butler: Equipment was improving. They were starting to buy some better engines, some new equipment. The old ones were tired and quite often you'd have some kind of breakdown where you wouldn't get one of the discharges working. You'd be running to look for another pumper to hook up to. When they did start to buy more modern equipment, it was laid out better, easier to work off of, both engines and trucks. They were easier to maneuver, a little better to drive. Gives you a little more room in there, better lay out for equipment.

That's when they introduced what they call a cross lay hose. We had pre-connected inch and a half hose that you could just step off the rig, grab and run. You didn't have to worry about hooking up. It was already hooked up. All you had to do was holler for your pump driver to give you water on that line. Just these little things here and there gave you the few extra seconds you needed, something to start making quicker hits. But the equipment definitely did start improving.

Cody: We had a Mack pumper. Of course everybody stood on the back at the time. No windshield, no covers, and it was a three hundred gallon tank, a thousand gallons a minute pumper. When I first went to Six Engine they had that rig with the high pressure pumps. It wasn't the John Bean. The John Bean was the International. We had the Mack, but it had the high pressure pump on it and Chief Donlon loved the high pressure. He loved it, so we used to use that. They used to put the fire out, but they never cooled anything off. You wouldn't see any fire, but you would be burnt. And he wanted you always to go in there. One thing about it, you always got the front of the building. You never had to stretch in because he wanted you to get right in front of the building. Someone else would have to feed you. But they didn't use much water. They only used like fifteen gallons a minute. Those things used to come out with such high pressure.

It worked. It did work, but they were no good for overhauling because what they did, they would put out the surface fire. But you didn't get enough water to cool the atmosphere. You just would have this steam build up. That's what was putting the fire out. Then you had to have ventilation

14

ahead of you because if you didn't, it was going to blow back on you and you were going to get burnt. A lot of guys got burnt. That's what we had first. Then the high pressure pump went out of service. It had the two booster reels. They both had high-pressure guns, but when that had gone out they never fixed it. We used that Mack for a while.

Then we got a LaFrance. It was Eighteen Engine's second piece. They gave it to us as a first piece. It had rapid water, but that never really worked. It was really a horrible rig. I remember it used to make such a horrible bouncing noise. It was very uncomfortable and used to snap you. We sent it to the shop and they found out there was nothing bolting it to the frame. All the bolts that hold it to the body or the chassis to the frame were just sheared off. Then we got that little Compac. There was no room to put anything. That was the first electronic siren. We were the first ones to get them.

Knight: Some of the equipment we had back then was old. I came on in '64. The first fire engine I drove was a 1947 Mack. That was the one Twenty-nine Engine had. They were antiques then for crying out loud.

McGovern: Twenty-seven at the time was two-piece with an old Ford hose wagon and at the time they had a Mack. Then right after that they got an FWD, which was the last one I think the city ever bought. But it was a real big heavy-duty FWD four-wheel drive. They gave it to Thirty-two Engine later and Twenty–seven got a new piece. All the spares at the time were the old LaSalles open cab snub-nosed. Any time you needed a spare that was what you used. They bought those during the war. You were hanging on the back step. The old LaSalles had a jump seat, one on each side. But if

15

you're one and four you had one guy on the back and two guys on the side. They were good though.

They put plywood over you right after I came on the job. That was after the riots. Some of them had it and some didn't. Then we had the Martin Luther King burnings in 1968 and they outfitted everybody with the plywood over the back

J. Cosby: Our apparatus was a Mack. It was a pretty old Mack, but it was good. It did the job. As a matter of fact it was better than a lot of the new equipment that they bought. It never stayed in the shop. It was a good piece of apparatus.

McDonnell: The engines all had that wooden piece of plywood across. That was just something they added to the rig. Probably Mack was the predominant type of engine. The city evidently bought apparatus whenever they needed them. At one time they bought a bunch of Macks, but then the next time they would buy an apparatus it could be from a different manufacturer. There wasn't any standard apparatus.

Pianka: When I went to Six Engine they had a Mack, a B3 Mack if I recall correctly. They had just gotten rid of the old high pressure. I think they changed the pumps. That's the way they operated because we had twin hoses on that so it had to be. That was nice. A lot of fun to drive, you'd whip that thing around. At the time everything was stick shift. Even the hook and ladders were all stick shift, which was good in the city. We rode on the back step. That's an experience. You say to yourself, "I don't think I'd ever want to do that again." But at the time you didn't know any better.

In certain ways it was fun. But it certainly is dangerous if you fall off the back of that thing. I'm surprised we didn't.

It's amazing. There were times when all three or four of us were on the back step, our hands through the loops, and nodding out half asleep. Because it's three o'clock in the morning, you're dead tired. I don't care. You could be doing fifty miles an hour; your eyes are closing on you. It's just that part of you realizes to hold onto that bar or that loop and you had that flexibility in your knees. You had to be a little flexed. Otherwise you get stiff armed right off the back step.

You had two and a half inch hose in the bed in front of you and you had three-inch hose. Those were the supply lines. To the left or the right, I forget, in our case I think it was to the left, you had inch and a half hose. When you're on the back step that was good. You pulled up to a fire. You could just pull it right off. That was a couple of extra seconds saved. When I first got there we didn't have any radio communications for the back step. Everything was by bells. They still had the bells on the fire engines at the time. If we had a working fire on the radio, if the captain knew we had a working fire, he would tap those bells real heavy. That way we knew they had a working fire so we could pull our boots up. Because if you didn't see the smoke; at least you had that notification. You'd pull up. You could pull everything right off the back.

We used to have a buzzer to let the driver in front know that we're ready to go or if there's an emergency, you'd press that buzzer to make it stop. Then you had firemen who started jury-rigging speakers, so we could hear what was going on over the radio. Because you're curious, you had to know what was going on.

We changed from the Mack to a Ward LaFrance with jump seats and Mattydale lays, but I don't know if we changed tactics. You just had to position your rig a little differently, that's all. I roll with the punches. If that's what we're going to do, that's what we do. I think most guys took stuff like that in stride.

What you saw maybe was the lack of quality maintenance or apparatus not being repaired properly or replaced on time, which goes on to this day by the way. That was frustrating. But just because you had a different color, what's the difference? I'm not a traditionalist in that respect. So, it's red one day, which is fine, yellow, and now we're going to go to white. I mean that's the way it goes. That didn't bother me. Even getting off the back step, ironically at the time I thought, "Oh Jesus." That sort of took away some of the wind out of your sail because you're not hanging on the back step with your scarf blowing in the breeze type thing. Now you're sitting in a pansy seat on the side of a rig. I mean, ironically, that's the way some of us looked at it. Because you're used to one thing and it was important at the time. Even that, you got used to it and now you're so spoiled with some of these newer rigs where we sit there. It's freezing outside, but you're inside and you're warm. It's a big difference. Believe me.

We had rapid water on the Ward. They explained what it was going to do. Rapid water was supposed to make water more slippery or something. A lot more water would flow for a given pressure. Really, we never used it that much. We used it a few times and it seemed to work better, but then they ran out of it or it cost too much money. So, we went back to the old fashion way of doing things. It never impressed me one way or another. It was just one of those fads that came and went.

T. Grehl: The fire engines were the old ones. After the riots they at least converted them. They put a cover over the back step, but prior to that there was just the back step open. It was cold in the winter, I'll tell you that. It was cold. When I came on, we did a lot of the highway runs. So, you'd be going down to Port Newark or the airport with the snow and it's minus whatever. You're hanging on the side with no protection. It was cold. It was really cold because you're going forty miles an hour on Route One.

Ryan: I was first assigned to One Engine. One Engine, we had a 1947 American LaFrance open top pumper with plywood over the top and over the back. There was no cab on the rig. It was quite an antique. Of course everything was standard shift in the fire department at the time. I had to be qualified on One Truck, which was the Snorkel, because they had just recently assigned several firefighters there who didn't know how to drive a standard transmission and the Snorkel was a standard transmission. So, if one of the old guys was out on One Truck, I was the driver of One Truck as well.

Pumps were centrifugal pumps. We didn't have any piston pumps anymore. I was surprised they didn't. Like I said, the first one I drove was a 1947 American LaFrance, which was pretty worn out. But it was still first line and that was it. We go driving down Broad Street and the kids would be laughing at us as if we were having a parade. I mean it looked like a very old fire engine. It was very small, had the plywood all over it.

The first rig at Eleven Engine I was on was an O cab Mack and it had a rounded hard cab. Then we had an R cab Mack that was painted the yellow-green. It was old Twenty Engine that got racked up and converted to diesel. That held up for a number of years. I rode on the back step until I went over to the truck. Eleven Truck had a cab. I think a year or so later Eleven Engine got a Continental and that had a cab, so that's putting it into the early '80's. And then we got one or two E-ones, as I recall. I was in Eleven

Truck for about a year and a half and then I transferred over to Rescue Squad. I was there for a couple of years and then back to Eleven Truck. And after that all the apparatus with the open cabs and the back steps were pretty much gone.

Carter: When I went to Eleven we had a '62 Mack. When that broke down they sent you 1946 Mack open cab pumper to ride around on. Let me tell you, you talk about feeling like the old iron men riding the wooden ship, blazing down Central Avenue hanging on the back of a Mack, siren wailing.

Luxton: We had the '72 "R" series Mack. I guess it had just come back from the accident with Twenty Engine because it had a fresh coat of yellow paint. The red was underneath it. That was a good rig. It had the plywood mask boxes on the side. You had the cover over the back step and you had the subway strap hanging bars on there. The captain and the driver were up front. There was really no room for a third guy up front because you had the gear shift there. He'd have to keep moving his legs out of the way. That was a real good rig.

Connell: Five Engine had just gotten a brand new Ward LaFrance when I got there. As a matter of fact, it got there maybe a week before I did. So, I had this new piece of apparatus to play with. I was one of the lucky ones.

Pignato: The engine was a Mack, probably one of the better engines at the time, probably to this date, probably more dependable. It was a Thermodyme I believe, a B-19, B-10 something like that. The truck was a Seagrave, red, tractor-trailer, which was nice. A little slow, but it was pretty good. It was a couple of years old when I got there and it was red until it died. It was always red. They never painted it yellow.

Langevin: Eighteen Engine was a two piece company. They had a B-model Mack. I'm not exactly sure what year it was and they had an International for their hose wagon.

Bisogna: Two old Macks, one was probably eight years older than the other. Twenty Engine's pumper was a red Mack and the hose wagon was a faded red Mack. No power steering, no power brakes, stick shifts, lifted me right off the floor when I went around a turn. The steering wheel was bigger than I was and you had to actually get up and pull on it. If I held on as I released it, it picked me right out of the seat. I had to use all my hundred and forty-five pounds to make a turn. So, you could appreciate some of these guys were big guys. We had those rigs the whole time I was there. We were on the back step hanging on for dear life. Keeping your knees bent.

Gesualdo: Apparatus at the time I came on was a '74 Mack, stick shift. No jump seats, just the rear step, you had to jump onto the rear step, hold onto the bar. I remember it having a make shift canopy with supports. They were bolted into the sides. Two pieces of two by four over our head and a little window type devise in the front to block the wind. The overhead obviously was to protect us. At that time when we used to respond to the Kretchner Homes a lot, we'd get a lot of debris thrown from the roofs and things like that, so we had the overhead protection. Ten Truck had a Seagrave tiller truck. Twenty-nine and Ten were both red, the way fire apparatus should be. I remember not wanting to lose it when I found out we were getting, I believe it was Six Engine's old rig, which was yellow and white. I remember feeling really bad about losing that Mack, but things change in the department rapidly.

Chapter Two: Trucks

Masters: The truck was an Ahrens-Fox truck, wooden ladder, seventy-five footer. They had all wooden ladders. Everything was spring operated. You had to use those handles to raise the aerial, to turn the turn table. Get the tiller man's seat off or else your aerial wouldn't go up.

Grehl: The trucks were the same with the aerial ladders. All of them were the tiller type trucks.

Vesey: They had some new and some older trucks. Three Truck had a Pirsch, Five Truck had a Pirsch. One Truck had a big hundred-foot aerial. It was a big dog. The other ones were hand-me-downs. Then they had a couple of new LaFrances. All the engines they were buying were LaFrance. They'd mix them up. A couple of Macks, those LaFrances with the cab ahead of the engine, then Six Engine got the Bean. They started to get new trucks in. They did stick with Pirsches. They brought Pirsches for a while. Then they went down to Florida.

Two Truck ended up with another monster up there. It had a big ladder on it. You felt like you were going up a stairwell. That's how wide the ladder was. Then they would dump most of the older stuff off on the slower companies. Recycle them. The Pirsches had an eighty-foot, two-section aerial ladder. Then they came out with those little metal ladders with the aerials, they would come in four sections. The old wooden ones were two sections. Some of those old ones, like the Ahrens-Fox, they had compressed air to take it out of the bed. Then you'd crank up the second section. They were only seventy-five foot ladders.

There were some that had springs. Seven Truck had one that was spring loaded. The bed ladder would whip up, then the fly would go out. Getting the fly out was all manual labor. The Pirsch was the best apparatus they ever bought, I guess, as far as service life, use, and dependability. I had to work with one for a long time. It was our favorite. The ladders were better.

Deutch: When I went to Five Truck we had a Peter Pirsch and we loved it. They had a good engine. They did the job. Very bad compartment space, but good with the ladders.

Wall: In Ten Truck we had a Pirsch Truck. It was a vehicle that the city had purchased from the department of the Navy at the conclusion of the Second World War. It was an old wooden aerial mounted on a Pirsch chassis. I was in the company probably less than a month because it was my first response to a fire and we were going down Frelinghuysen Avenue. The driver was on the wrong side of the street at the curb by Weequahic Park and traffic was coming in his direction. He attempted to apply the brakes, skidded and put us between poles shearing off both fenders. We didn't have the Pirsch for about a year. They gave us a 1928 Ahrens-Fox with a spring loaded aerial. The first kick went up so high and then the air tanks took over, but to put out the fly you did it by hand wheel. Which was a lot of fun, I mean you really looked forward to putting the aerial out.

McGee: When you responded on the truck, you rode on the side, standing up usually by the turntable. That way you could see and you were high in case they hit you. There's a rail around the turntable that you held onto. In the beginning there were quite a few wooden ladder trucks with a spring raise.

They were some of the older trucks that were still in service and you might get as a spare. Most of the newer trucks had metal ladders. I don't think many of them were a hundred feet. They might have been seventy-five feet as oppose to a hundred feet. They were pretty much the same operation, hydraulic operation, tractor-trailers with a tillerman.

Stoffers: We had a seventy-five foot, two-section aerial. The metal aerials they have today are three and four sections. When they backed it into the firehouse, the end of the ladder would have to go into the kitchen door, so they could close the doors up front. That one was spring- loaded. When you raised the aerial, you'd set the truck up and you'd pop it. It would go up and they had cranks that you'd turn at the side. You'd have to watch it and hope that you have it at the top of the lift. You didn't want it to go up and then start down again.

Dunn: When I came on the fire department, our aerial ladders were eight-five feet on our ladder trucks. We have the hundred and hundred and tens now. The real change in the truck company that I can really point to is the fact that we went from the senior aerial which is a tractor tailor type to a straight body truck. Was it an advancement? It's supposed to be the state of the art, but in the residential districts where I'm working now I find that the tractor-trailers were more mobile. They could get around a little better than the stuff we're using today. I often wonder if anybody who makes fire engines ever really sits down and looks at what we have to work with as far as the make up of a major city is concerned. Do they compare that to what we're sold and what everybody's buying?

Carragher: When I came on the job Two Truck had the first aluminum ladder, a hundred-foot aluminum.

Haran: When I came on in '61 we had old wooden ladders. Six Truck had an old wooden ladder. We used to call it the stick. That's where that expression came from. Throw the stick up. Because that's what it was an old wooden aerial ladder.

Highsmith: The apparatus, we had hook and ladders. I think we might only have one in the city now. I'm not sure. But everything was hook and ladder with the tiller man on the back. It was a nice sight to see those guys riding down the street with the tiller on the back, the front going one way, the back going the other way. It was really something to see.

Butler: We still had some wooden ladders when I came on. When you went out, you rinsed off under the rigs if it was a nasty day. A little rain or something, you didn't worry too much, but quite often you did wipe the rig when you came back. The ladders were washed according to whether you used them or not. If they got dirty you rinsed them, but you didn't wipe the ground ladders off. You did wipe the rig down somewhat. You weren't going to go to a full dress parade the next day, but you did wipe what you could. That was pretty much understood. Today I think the dust and dirt on half the rigs is what's holding them together and keeping them running.

Apparatus have improved today to the point where on the newest apparatus the men are fully enclosed, the driver, officer, and all the riders. When I first came on everything was wide open. All you had around you was a cab and some side windows, windshield and side windows. You didn't even have a roof over your head. You just sat out in the elements. I mean going to fires, rain, snow, whatever, ninety-five degree sun you were sitting wide open on the apparatus. Not until the riots came along in '67, where they were scrambling to get a couple of pieces of half inch plywood to form an inch thick piece over your head. Certain guys were even putting them on themselves, grabbing anything they could because we were getting really pelted with all kinds of stuff off of roofs. The city tried to scramble as much as they could, but a lot of the men just went out and got three quarter inch or a couple of half inch pieces together and tied them, nailed them, bolted them anyway they could to cover at least the cab area where the guys were riding.

Cody: There was a spare aerial. I don't know how old it was. It was like something from the '30s that they put out. This thing had an eighty-five foot ladder. A wooden ladder and we had it a couple of times there. In order for us raise the aerial you released a pedal and the spring engaged and it shot this thing up. To stop it you had a rotating disk with a brake shoe. You pulled on this thing and it would grab the brake shoe and you would stop this ladder. Then you'd crank out your fly. We didn't have it for long, but it was a spare that the city used at that time. It was pretty old. So we really can't complain now with what we have because you can't compare, could never compare. Fortunately we never used that at a fire.

Garrity: When I went to Nine Truck in 1978, I was used to a tractor trailer hook and ladder and this was the first rear mount truck in the city. I could never judge where the truck should be to use the ladder. You'd spot the ladder from behind. Well, the turntable was now thirty some odd feet behind you. I always thought the drivers were going past the building. I used to say, "Stop! Stop!" and they'd go, "No, no Cap, no. We have to get by the building to use the ladder."

That was the only major change, but it was a big one for me, resisting change. When I went up there I said, "I don't like this truck. Don't like this truck." After I was there about a month, rear mount aerial ladders were the best thing that ever happened because you could do a lot of things with them you couldn't do with a tractor-trailer. If you can get down the street, all you have to do is raise the ladder out of the bed. You can shoot it straight over the cab. There were a lot of things you could do with it that you couldn't do with a tractor-trailer. But that was a big step for me to be able to figure that one out. I had a lot of trouble with that one. Bobby Langevin used to think I was nuts. "Is there something wrong with you?" Of course, they had the Snorkel first and then they got this thing. They were the only ones who had it. They knew exactly what to do with it.

The yellow fire engines were the worst thing I ever heard. Yellow fire engine, whoever heard of a yellow fire engine? It's supposed to be red. We hated the yellow. I remember getting flagged down one day on Broad Street. The woman thought we were a bus. That's the truth. She flagged us down on Broad Street, thought we were a bus. She looked and asked, "What kind of bus is this?" "It's not a bus. It's a fire engine." And even she didn't like it.

Wargo: When I first came on, our truck was an American LaFrance. It was a hook and ladder, articulated. We had wooden ladders on it and an open cab with jump seats on the side. The equipment was kept in good shape because if you went out on a run and came back, you would pull the ladders and equipment all off and wipe them down. Wipe the wheel wells in the truck. While you were cleaning them you were checking them to see if there was anything broken or any of the equipment was damaged, so it served two purposes. You did that whenever it got wet. If you went out and it got rainy out or it was snowing or you went in the mud or something, you washed that apparatus right away. Wiped it down, kept it in good shape.

With the aluminum ladders, you got away from that. Today they'll pull out a ladder in a lot of the companies and it looks like it hasn't been out of there in years. It probably hasn't. And that's from not checking them. They become dirty, especially today with the diesels. It gets up into the ladder compartment of the new trucks and it sticks like glue. So you have to pull them out, check them out.

Prachar: We had an old Pirsch for an aerial. There's nothing like a cold winter night riding down the street, hanging onto the aerial, freezing in rain and everything. The equipment then was nothing compared to today and yet you have the guys today hollering that they have to sit inside the bucket or whatever. We even had a wooden aerial at the time when I came on assigned to Six Truck that was still being used as a spare.

Comparing equipment, there's no comparison. The older equipment, slow as it was, you had to know where to place it. As far as a truck company, jackknife it. Your placement was your major thing, how and where, when, wires, whatever. Today with your high aerials with the high side rails, you can't get through a lot of spaces. Then you only had a foot of aerial to play with. You rode up the runner the whole way. So, you could slide through a lot of close wires.

McDonnell: The type of equipment in the city, there wasn't a standard make with the truck companies. It was more eclectic. Everybody had their own. We had a High Ranger Snorkel. Who had a Pirsch. Somebody else had a Ward LaFrance. I don't know if it was in Six Truck. They had their own. I don't know what it was. It might have been the only fire apparatus made like that, but we still had Pirsches. We had Pirsches around. There were a couple of wooden aerial ladders still around. We had a spare with a wooden ladder. The spare apparatus we were using at that time were made in the '40s.

They had aluminum aerial ladders that had open tillers. The cages and all of that came after. Those apparatus didn't have them at all. The apparatus manufacturer didn't make them. Those cages and stuff that were on the rigs, the fire department made them. They were just things that they added on. The truck just had the tiller wheel, a little windshield, and a little piece of canvas clothe to keep the wind from blowing off your coat and that was it. You used to have to break them apart and take the steering wheel out. That little box, that thing they built around the tiller seat was something they built after the riots, protection from thrown objects. That was all from post-riot, riot-renaissance architecture. They went from just doing it Rube Goldberg style to being manufactured that way.

Especially with the trucks, there were longer periods between the times they bought a truck as opposed to an engine. They just evidently bought whoever was there at the time. Whatever they liked if they had it or whoever was the low bidder. There were aluminum ladders, steel ladders. There were actually three section aerials. They were longer. In fact, at that time most of the aerials were three sections. The trucks were longer. The four section aerials came in probably in the mid-'70s. That's when they started buying and going for four section aerials. It gave them a shorter rig.

Everything was open underneath. There were no cabinets. There were just open beds where they kept all the tools. The ladder bed and then underneath was a big open bed. You kept all the tools in there.

When I made captain, we still had hook and ladders, the old trucks with the tiller that you took apart. When they went to the tiller cabs that extended along the back, they were murder. The vibration would kill you. Oh, God. Punch the hell out of you. It was murder back there, bouncing like crazy. Especially the streets in Newark with eight million pot holes never getting repaired.

Then we went to the Jimmy Carter rig. There was a Carter era idea that it was wasteful for fire departments to buy apparatus manufactured just for the fire department. They said it would be much cheaper and just as efficient to use mass produced apparatus. We got one. The only one they had in Newark. We got an old trailer with the regular truck tractor. They gerrymandered this thing. They made it into a rig and it was the biggest mistake. You could walk to the alarm as fast as we could get to it with that damn rig. It would take a half an hour to build up speed. In the city you go down to the corner and you have to slow down. You'd get up to ten miles an hour. At the light you have to slow down, stop, and start all over again. The thing was terrible. It was a really stupid idea. I don't know what geniuses came up with that idea, but it certainly didn't work. It was a blundering half. It was a useless rig. People would be shouting, "Come on, there's a fire! What are you doing?" He's got it floored. It doesn't go any faster. "What the hell are you waiting for?"

That was in-between the regular hook and ladder and the straight rigs with the four section aerials. And the ladders changed, they got a lot bigger and a lot stronger. When I first came on the job, we had aluminum ladders. They were four sections and smaller. They weren't as wide. When you used to get to the top section, the rails were only like six inches high. When they were at low angles it was tough to climb them. It was almost like a hands and knees type of thing. Then they got to the four sections. The ladders were bigger. The rails were higher. The ladder was actually wider and sturdier. They didn't move as much. They still moved, but not as much.

When I was a captain I used to try to emphasize, put both rails on the building. Because those old ladders with the one rail on the building, by the time you got up there it was wavering. Those things used to move. They weren't real sturdy. I used to hate that. The other thing was when you got off the ladder and it sprang. You're not supposed to leave the ladder on the building. You're supposed to position the ladder so it's a few inches above. So that it's your weight that brings it down. Supposedly equalizes the tensions on the ladder. But the ladder springs on you. You have one leg on the roof and all of the sudden the ladder's moving. You could be laying on the ground, worried about compressing your bones down there. They improved in that way. The rigs definitely improved.

The only thing I didn't like about the straight rigs is you're losing the maneuverability. It's tougher to get the aerial up. It's tougher to position it, as opposed to having a hook and ladder where you could jack knife. They were much more maneuverable than the newer rigs even though the newer rigs are shorter than the old ones. They're definitely not as maneuverable and it was a lot tougher to position the apparatus, to get the ladder up. In that sense it wasn't an improvement. I don't know how they even get down the streets, like Down Neck, you have this big, monstrous truck.

The last one we got was an E-One. We got one a couple of days before I retired. Those things are huge, enormous. The cab is a lot better, not great, but better than that Jimmy Carter rig. I'm a skinny guy and I was cramped in that seat. They had the big console with the engine underneath it and the driver's seat and this little, tiny seat on the other side. You couldn't do anything. You couldn't put your mask on. You couldn't do anything in there; it was so damned cramped. I don't know how a heavy guy sat in there. It was like the bucket seats on the rigs now for the guys. They're cramped in there.

There have been a lot of changes. We went from being outside, riding on the turntable or back by the tillerman to eventually getting a whole enclosed cab for the men. It's a lot different. You don't freeze your butt off in the winter, holding on, curling up, trying to keep the wind from chilling your bones. The apparatus changed quite a bit, a big evolution.

Melodick: We had a hook and ladder. I was on the job probably less than a week. We had a fire on Sixteenth Avenue and Fourteenth Street. A couple of the guys got hurt and my captain said to me, "You're going to have to drive." We had a Seagrave. To me the nose of this thing was so long and I'm saying, "I have to drive? I have no idea how to drive this thing." The captain was a really nice guy and he said, "You'll be all right." All I kept saying was, "Oh God, how am I going to back this into the firehouse?" We had a long drive back from the fire.

I got lucky. I drove it, somebody else was tillering because I had no idea how to do that either, but I was the only guy left. I had to drive. The other guy was tillering. All I remember was getting back and all I kept saying was, "Please, I hope we don't go out. I hope we don't go out." I didn't want to drive. I said to myself, "I have no clue what I'm doing here." All I remember him telling me was, "Make sure when you pull out of Nine Truck, you go past the door. Make sure the cab clears or otherwise you're going to take part of the building with you." So, I said, "Okay." He kept telling me to go to the center of Avon Avenue, the white line, then start turning. Sure enough we had one or two runs. I was all nervous.

Pianka: We had a 1953 Pirsch hook and ladder. It was a hundred foot metal aerial ladder. Everything was metal at that point. Once in a while, if you got a spare ladder, I remember seeing a couple of wooden ones around. But predominantly they were metal. The lifesaving net is still on the truck right behind the cab, sitting up there. The tiller seat was like a break away where when you got to the fire, you lifted the wheel off and you broke down the back end. It was fairly simple to do. Take that off and then you could raise the ladder.

You rode one and five. Driver and tillerman went to the roof to ventilate. The captain and the other two men would go inside with hooks, axes, whatever they needed. There were no jump seats. You hung onto the side. Everything was wide open. During the winter it's cold. It's bitter cold.

They put a plywood roof on the rigs, but the men weren't covered. The tiller had a little protection. One of the guys used to crawl in behind the tiller. They had about a ten-foot section that over hung on the ladder. He just didn't like it cold. He would crawl behind the tillerman and lay in the bed of the ladder. I mean, really, it was cold.

I remember the first time I went out as a tillerman. That was a big deal. "All right, now we're going to take you out. We're going to train you how to do this thing." Going forward is no problem because it's simple. You just turn the same way you're going. The hard part was backing in because that thing had to go opposite to the way you thought it had to go. Essentially, if you wanted the tiller, backing in, to go left, you pushed with

34

your left hand. If you wanted to go right, you pushed with your right hand. After a while it came naturally.

After being certified on this thing, one morning I come in and sure enough it's going to be the first day I'm going to tiller. This is my first day. A box comes in like eight o'clock. Eight o'clock, you're not even ready on a normal day. Holy Christ! Now you jump up there and we went out the door. There were two humps on the inside of the door going out. I hit that. I rammed it. I bounced off that because I'm nervous. I'm not thinking. The fire is up on Blum Street and Sixteenth Avenue. We go Waverly to Springfield, make a left, and go up Springfield Avenue. You could see the smoke. Turn into Blum, Frankie Mastroeni was driving.

Blum is narrow. He guns it. I never got back in time, bounced off about three cars. I looked back. Chrome was flying in the air. We get to the fire. The joint is ripping. Put the fire out. I said, "Frankie, what'd you do to me?" He said, "I forgot it was you. I'm sorry. Don't worry, we'll take the ride." Went back there, nobody ever reported it. Nobody said anything.

T. Grehl: I'm going to guess we had a Pierce. Only for the fact that somebody told me they heard Five Truck was a Pierce and I remember us having the same hook and ladder as Five Truck. Everything was basically open. The tiller cab was removable. You had to take the wooden cab and swing it over. It was on hinges. The tillerman sat on the ladder with a seat and the steering wheel that could be removed. You had to flip open the thing and take out the steering wheel before the driver came out and started raising the aerial. All the tools and everything were exposed and underneath the bed of the ladder, the masks and everything. Everything was exposed. There were no compartments.

When we raised the aerial up, we positioned the same basic way you do today, but then you had a pin and you pulled out the outriggers, the jacks, and then manually cranked them down. We had a pad to put down under them to protect the macadam. It was a pain in the neck because you had to manually pull those things out. Today they come out hydraulically. It wasn't too bad then because if you parked too close to a car, maybe you didn't put down the outrigger or you only put it out six inches or you slid it out and still got out the correct distance. Today these things come out feet. If you don't give yourself room, you're going to go through a car. So we didn't have that to worry about. The ladders were nowhere near what they are today. They were slower and just totally different in that respect.

Carter: When I learned to tiller, we had a '62 Pirsch at Eleven Truck. Cost them a bundle of money teaching me to tiller, to back into the firehouse. Herbie Foster's grandson was there the day I was finally going to graduate as a tillerman. Everybody teaches you their way to tiller, but you have to find the one that works. So I'm backing in and I'm nice and even coming in. I just pushed it the wrong way. Instead of pushing left, I pushed right. I took out three lockers, the side door, and a window of the firehouse. Herbie's little grandson looks up at his grandfather and says, "Hey, that was fun. Is Mr. Harry going to do that again?" To this day, the kid is now in his twenties, he still remembers Mr. Harry learning to tiller. But that's when you had the old Pirsches. You're sitting on a milk box because there was no seat. You had to learn how to pull the steering wheel out of the tiller and spring the seat. I don't know. I just felt more like a fireman.

Langevin: When I came on the job, a lot of the equipment, now that I look back at it, was outdated or ancient. I was lucky enough to go to Nine Truck.

They had a fairly new piece of apparatus, but it's since proved to be probably useless. It was an eighty-five foot Mack snorkel.

We were known as a ground ladder company because of where Nine Truck was. The neighborhood tended to have a lot of trees and overhead wires. We couldn't maneuver the boom without getting tangled up, so we usually went for the thirty-five footer right off the bat. If we knew we didn't have a shot, we always went for the thirty-five footer to the roof and then carried our tools with us. If we put the boom up, we always carried a hook and an ax in the basket. It was easy to put the saw in the basket and raise it to where we had to go. But a lot of times we just didn't have the room or it would take too long. By the time we get the outriggers set and the boom up, the fire would be knocked down. They wouldn't need it. So, we threw a lot of ground ladders.

For where they had it stationed, the Snorkel was a waste of time, only because of the make-up of the neighborhood, a lot of trees, a lot of wires. At the same time, Truck One stationed downtown had a Snorkel. Downtown it would work very well because there were very few overhead wires and things like that. They could get it in operation. We were also special called to major fires a lot because we had that piece. They basically would use us as a water tower.

Ricca: On the old aerial, you used to stand on the turn table and there was a little, thin bar, looked like a clothes hanger, you'd hang on to that. The coldest thing in the world is you having a run to the Burg and riding up from down below. You'd ride backwards so the wind wouldn't freeze you to death. Then coming back from a fire was the same thing. Just getting back to the firehouse was an adventure. Everything was slippery.

Then they came with the trucks that had the jump seats for two, but there still were guys hanging all over the place. The old saying was step up from the runner board to ride because at the runner board you were at the level of a traffic accident. So you always wanted to stay higher than the traffic which was great, but in the summer time with the trees blooming and you ended up on a tree lined street, you'd get whacked in the head under every branch as you went by.

Eventually we had the Seagrave and three or four guys could fit in the cab. Nobody rode up front unless it was an ice cold day or we were coming back from a job because we would mask up on the way there and we couldn't in the cab. Another thing, when you didn't ride in the jump seat, you got a good view of the fire. With these new rigs now, it's hard to place the aerial. It's hard to see what you have. On Twelve Engine, you're riding backwards. There's not even a jump seat that lets you see forward. So, basically, you're getting on the scene not knowing what you have.

I remember the spares, getting an old Pirsch. There was no roof. They just had the wood shield that they put on after the riots. You were able to almost stand up and spot the aerial as you drove into the building. The only thing I like about the enclosed rigs is the guys stay warm coming back from a run or on a three hundred.

Chapter Three: Turnout Gear

Fredette: We had a leather helmet. Mine was eight bucks when I came in. We paid for everything. There was no clothing allowance or anything. Then later on the city came along with inner soles for us to avoid stepping on nails. But when we came in we bought all of our equipment. We had no equipment at all. We had just a helmet, boots, and a rubber coat, then our night rig. We always had them because at Six Engine if you didn't have a night rig you wouldn't make the apparatus.

Vetrini: I went in as a temporary. When I went in as a temporary I didn't have the rubber goods, but naturally I had to get them. In a day or so I had to go up and get them. When we went on as regulars I already had equipment, but the new fellows who hadn't been on before had to get it. We were up to school, so naturally they spent the day to get them outfitted with the rubber goods. Anytime there was a multiple alarm, the recruits would automatically be taken to the fire. You paid five bucks to join the credit union. That was the only way we got our equipment. We had no money. At that time, your complete outfit, rubber goods, uniform, and everything was maybe seventy-five dollars, big money, seventy-five dollars.

The rubber coats we had at the time had just a thin felt lining in them. There was no attachment to put in an inner lining. Then later on they did have them. What we did was wear our old army jackets underneath the rubber coat. In the summer time you just didn't have the jacket on, but in the wintertime you needed it on. Some of us had these little GI wool vests that they used in tanks with the sheepskin lining.

We always had our rubber goods on. If an officer saw you without your equipment on, you were definitely in trouble. We were supposed to be dressing ourselves as soon as we got on the rig. You would have your coat lying there and you would throw it on. Then you would jump into your boots. It wasn't a matter of putting your boots on while you were rolling. They were right there at the step. So you were fully clothed so to speak by the time you got to the fire. There was no excuse not to have your equipment on.

Redden: I had a helmet naturally and of course at that time the helmet had to be fitted, so you didn't have a helmet right away. There was one of the old timers in Two Engine whose helmet fit me. It was big enough to fit me. I used his helmet and I got fitted up in Cairns for a helmet. I guess it took about a month to get it. Then I had a rubber coat, which I bought at Cairns, and also rubber boots. Nobody ever thought of gloves. It wasn't the he-man attitude. It was just that people didn't think of gloves.

Masters: We went to Cairns. They were off of Central Avenue there by Bally Street. I had a helmet, rubber coat, and rubber boots. That was it. You bought your gloves, but there were no bunker pants or anything like that. Now, they have everything. The helmet's a leather helmet. I still have it in my garage. I got an extra-long coat because when you stretched the end of the raincoat would come up. My captain, De Paul, says, "Oh, I can't work with a long coat." So, he cuts it short. When he pulled something his boots always got full of water. His coat never covered his boots. We used to go to a store on Bradford Place for fire equipment. That's where we all went for shirts and pants and all that.

F. Grehl: It was a rubber coat and a regular leather helmet, which they changed now to plastic and Nomex coats. The boots are basically the same

40

except they're steel toed and arches. When we were changing from regular coats to the Nomex coats we had a job around change of shift time. We took a company up the front. The next thing you know I look up at the third floor and I see windows getting broken. The tact unit is up there and they're ventilating. Then, I hear a scream. There's nothing but flames coming out of the third floor windows they just broke. I know there's a whole company in there. I ran upstairs and I catch a few of the guys coming down the stairs, scrambling. The captain is coming down the stairs and he was hurting. He got burnt. I had to write a big report.

At the time, two things stood in my mind. One was the coats. Some guys had the rubber coats, some had the canvas coats, and another guy had the Nomex coat on. Some of the guys had long hair. It went down over their ears. They all had masks on, which was fortunate because that saved their respiratory system from being burned. They all had gloves except for the captain. When he saw it coming at him instinctively he put his hands up over his face. That's when he got his hands burnt. It was a flash over. Nothing happened to the ears of all those guys with long hair. Their ears weren't singed or anything. Their hair got singed, but their ears were good. The ears of the guy who had the short haircut were burnt.

Now we get to the coats, the rubber goods. Because they were a good company, they all had their boots pulled up all the way. So, nobody's legs got burnt. The coats they had on, nobody got burnt in and around the crotch area. No burns on the body anywhere. No matter what type of coat they had on, nobody was burnt. The only ones who were burnt were the guy who didn't have long hair and the captain's hands. So, the coats made no difference at all.

I had to go to a meeting when they were going to make this a regulation. I said I was opposed to the coats because they leaked like a sieve. You got soaking wet. I said, "No, I opposed them. Your idea and your principal are great, but we're getting soaking wet. The probability of you getting hurt, cold, pneumonia, and everything else is a lot greater than you getting burned. Nobody got burned in this fire." They said, "Yes, but that was just a flash over. If you were in that heat for a longer period of time, the coat would help you." I said, "What you're really forgetting is you're putting this on the guy and he already has all these plastics. The one thing that is most important in your life is to be able to breathe. If you can't breathe it doesn't make any difference what you have on or whether you get burnt or not. It's all plastic. All around your face on that mask is plastic and plastic has the lowest ignition temperature of all these things. So, you're going to burn that first. Aren't you concerned about that?" He's concerned about the guy's coat. We couldn't convince him. They went with it anyway, probably for their own protection, liability wise.

Vesey: We bought everything, bought the helmet, the boots, the rubber coat. The canvas coats came out later. You had a choice. They accepted both, the rubber coat or the canvas coat. The canvas coat was not as waterproof as the rubber coats, but they were a lot cooler. When they let us use them, I bought one. They were good. They had a lining you could take out. Then the boots, leather inner soles and so forth. The helmets are leather from Cairns. Gloves were optional. If you wanted to wear gloves you got an old pair of cotton, painter's gloves. If you had an old pair of gloves, you brought them in. Some guys wore mittens. You had to wear something. Everything is wet and slippery, cold.

McCormack: When I first came on the job it wasn't really mandatory that you wear rubber goods when you went to a fire. You had to have rubber goods. You bought rubber coats, boots, and a leather helmet. When I say it wasn't mandatory, there weren't any stringent regulations, hard fast regulations when you were mandated to wear your rubber coat and boots. Particularly in the summer time, a lot of firemen would simply say, "That coat's too hot." and they wouldn't wear their coats. Most of them wore their helmets and most of them wore their boots, but many of them would go into a working fire with khaki pants and a blue shirt on. They would work that way through the entire fire. They'd come out soaking wet.

The rubber coats didn't have any liners in them or anything like that. They were unlined rubber shells, which could go over everything. A lot of them were in pretty bad states of disrepair. They were torn, ripped, shredded, and everything else. And guys didn't want to buy new ones because they cost money and in those days the city wouldn't buy you clothes or give you clothes. So it came down to your own pocket. You didn't even get a clothing allowance in those days. So the guys tried to stretch those coats as long as they could. Given the fact that even in a busy company you might only go to a few fires a year, it wasn't all that imperative so to speak that you have coats. The officers didn't even insist on it.

The winter firefighting gear of a lot of guys in the late '40s and early '50s was surplus army and navy equipment. I remember seeing firemen in those days wearing khaki full-length overcoats with brass buttons on them. And I remember seeing them with a fireman's helmet on and that coat and rubber boots and a hook pulling ceilings in a building. They would say that the wool was warm even when it was wet. They wore the coat for that reason. I suspect the real reason they did it was because they didn't want to buy a rubber coat. They bought the Army coat home from the service with them, so they wore that. I remember seeing many of them wearing those coats for years. Many years after World War II and into the '50s they were still wearing that type of coat.

Gloves were a no-no. You were a sissy if you wore gloves. The first fireman who wore gloves was laughed at throughout the department. They called him the kid glove fireman. He was some type of sissy because he couldn't work without gloves. You had to work bare handed. There was no such thing as "Fireball" gloves or any kind of gloves like that to keep you warm in the wintertime. They used to sell, in Cairn's, a sort of hard coarse mitten. It was a hard knitted wool thing. We were told even if these mittens got soaking wet on the most freezing cold day in the winter time; you could take them off; wring them out; put them back on again; and they would keep your hands from freezing.

Most of us had a pair of mittens at that time in our pockets for cold, severe winter weather. But the idea of wearing gloves to protect you from cuts was a concept that hadn't even come into the fire department. Breaking glass and cuts and stuff like that, that was not why you wore gloves. The only reason you wore gloves was to keep your hands warm in the wintertime. My wife knitted me a pair of navy blue worsted mittens out of some kind of tight wool stuff. I had those gloves for I bet twenty-five years in my coat pocket. I always carried them with me.

The leather helmets required an awful lot of maintenance. Every single year you had to paint your leather helmet. You had to rub it down with steel wool or sandpaper. They were painted with black enamel or white in the case of the chiefs. You had to rub it down and get all the loose scaly paint off. Of course many of these helmets were in fires so the paint would bubble on the helmet or deteriorate. You had to rub them down and paint

44

them. We did this for the annual inspection. You had to use a black stove type enamel on them. That was a yearly thing you had to maintain.

Over the life of the helmet, the helmet would deteriorate to the point where it would start to change its shape. The brim would bend down in the back and instead of being a nice curve it would almost develop a right angle. The helmet was constructed in pieces, like sections stitched together. Sometimes these sections would become dimpled and cave in at the crown of the helmet. Some guys used one helmet for their entire career on the fire department, which could span like 40 years, given the fact that we didn't have as many fires as we do today. Every few years you had to take the helmet back to Cairns. They would reconstruct the helmet and send it back to you. Put a new eagle on the front to hold the front piece because we were prone to breaking windows out with our helmets. The helmet required a lot of maintenance, where these plastic helmets today need practically no maintenance what so ever. You don't have to paint them. You don't have to do anything with them.

Masterson: You had to have the leather inserts in the boots, solid leather. That was very important with those people. They checked on that all the time. Inspections, you had to have them out and show them in those days. I can understand. You take them out and look at them. Boy, how they were scarred up by nails and stuff. Coats, you would want a shorter coat in an engine company. In a truck you would probably want a longer one. The Midwestern was a good coat. It had a felt lining in it. It was long. So that would keep the water more or less out of your boots. But I had both of them.

You wore gloves after you learned. You learned the hard way. I got more cuts. In winter time, I had a box of old gloves, a cardboard box in my locker. Everyone knew they were there because you always needed gloves. Especially since you don't know what you're grabbing inside. You don't know; windows, glass, and hot metal. You don't know what you're touching, electric wires. A couple of guys without gloves were plain stupid. In the winter time they'd be so damn cold, sometimes. My hands get cold. That's why I used to wear mittens if I had them. Mittens were better than gloves.

But normally you always had to wear gloves. You were crazy not to wear gloves because you'd get so beat up working on the roof with that metal. I had no gloves on one time. I broke out a sky light. I got a cut on the hand, but I don't know how I did it. I just banged it. I don't think that thing healed yet. You bought the cheapest they had. Who knows what kind? Any workman's gloves, something that would dry out. We used to take cans, vegetable cans, take the both ends out, put them in the gloves, put them on the radiator and dry them. That's about the best way, so you can get the insides dried out.

Wall: I didn't even have my own rubber goods for the first few months I was on the job. I was a cop with two kids at the time. I had just laid out over the previous year more than two hundred bucks for police uniforms because you had to buy everything except your gun for the police. A guy I was partners with a lot in the Fourth Precinct says to me, "Come on over. This job stinks. You don't like it. I don't like it." I said, "I can't afford it. If I go home and tell my wife I have to lay out another couple of hundred bucks for fire uniforms, she going to throw me out into the street." So, his brother was in Ten Engine at the time. We go down to see him. He says, "I'll lend you some of my spare stuff." He lent me a beat up helmet, a rubber coat that came down to my calf, and even a pair of boots that didn't fit. For about six months that was my turnout gear on the Newark Fire Department. Until I decided I was going to stay and I bought my own.

At that time it was a rubber, fleece-lined coat. They were very uncomfortable, very hot. And if you got near a fire, you got very burned. Leather helmets, of course, which persisted all the way through until the '70s. When I went to the Squad, a lot of truckmen and Squad guys bought canvas gear because it was warmer in the winter. We weren't exposed to as much water as engine company guys were. For a long time I wore canvas gear, until they came out with the Nomex stuff in the late '70s.

Smart guys wore gloves. The old timers thought you were a sissy if you put gloves on. We were too smart and said, "Ten fingers looks go. It's balanced." I wore leather driver's gloves for the most part with mittens in the winter.

When I was a captain, there was a synthetic material that Janesville made. It was a lot lighter than the rubber, a lot more breathable, and it kept you dry.

Freeman: Midwestern was the coat. It was rubber. It had a winter lining, which you could snap in and take out in the summer time. The helmets were leather and the boots were Siren boots. I wore the leather work-gloves, the little thin white ones? A lot of guys wore those. There was no regulation on gloves. Then I wore heavier leather gloves because glass would go right through those work gloves. I got a cut on my wrist once because glass went right through the glove. You could get slivers of glass in you. Everybody I knew used gloves. I don't see how you couldn't. You still had hot water coming down from fires and handling hose and stuff like that. There may have been some guys who didn't, but everybody who I knew did. In fact, they told me to use gloves. So I'm pretty sure they used gloves.

McGee: I don't care what they say. They can have the Nomex. Those rubber coats were good. You stayed dry in those rubber coats. They weren't as heavy as this new stuff. I know it's fireproof and all that baloney, but the old equipment was better. The helmets were much better than the plastic helmets we have now. They were leather helmets. It almost looked like you baked them after a while because they would get all crusty and bent up. They were also very protective. I personally was hit on the head with a couch thrown from a second floor window, knocked to the ground with those helmets. I didn't have any problem at all with it.

I thought the equipment was good because it was light. One of the biggest problems that I saw with the equipment later was it became too cumbersome, too heavy. You would literally be so exhausted from sweating just wearing the stuff and then you would be going into the superheated atmosphere. It was much more difficult to take the heat than it was with this other stuff. I liked the older stuff. To tell the truth, I didn't wear gloves. But there were no regulations requiring you to wear them.

Stoffers: Rubber coat, leather helmet, boots. Other than the rubber coat, you'd have a foul weather jacket or something like that. Our work uniform was the blue shirts and the khaki pants, but captains wore blue pants and a white shirt.

Denvir: I had my old boots from Public Service. They weren't good, but they were a pair of boots. I didn't have to lay out the money for them. I bought the rubber coat. I forget where I bought it, might have been Cairns. You had to go up there. Everybody wore what they wanted. There was no uniform coat that everybody had. Some had cotton duck turnout coats. Some guys had rubber, whatever they wanted, back in those days. The helmets were Cairns leather. They were good. The ones we have today are terrible. They're ridiculous. I don't know how they get away with it.

Charpentier: Prior to us being sworn in we were told that we were definitely going to be appointed on the first of March, that we should get our rubber goods and a work uniform. Well I had mine because I was with the Bell and Siren and I was an auxiliary. I had all my stuff. But most of them borrowed or bought. A lot of them didn't have theirs yet. I don't know whether it was financial or size or what, but a lot of them were using the turn-out gear of different tours. The older firemen from the different tours were lending them theirs until they got their own.

You definitely had to have it. If you walked into your assignment and you didn't have it, you had to scrounge from somebody else. At that time we had to buy all our own equipment. A lot of guys were reluctant. "Hey, I paid for this. Why should I let you borrow it? Maybe you'll rip it or something." There was very little swapping going on. But you definitely had to have turnout gear before you even rode the apparatus.

Smith: We had the leather helmet that was fitted just to you. I had a Midwestern that was strictly rubber with a liner inside and I had the hip boots. The coats were longer, much longer. They went below your knee. We used to take them to a shoemaker. He would turn it up and take a hem in it. If your coat got ripped, you could take it to a gas station to have a vulcanized patch put on, the same with your boots. I never liked those plastic helmets. A porch fell on me one time at a fire off Elizabeth Avenue. A big twelve by twelve beam came down, hit me in the head, pinned me down on the ground. When it hit the helmet, it bounced. If I had a plastic helmet on me, the force would have been transmitted through the helmet right onto my neck. It would have snapped it.

Carragher: You bought all your own protective gear, all your own work clothes. Everything was on your own. When I came on the job, any turnout coat you wanted you put on. Boots you could get what you wanted. Helmet, you had to wear those Cairns leather, but gloves, you could put on anything you wanted, whatever kind of mitten, whatever you were comfortable with. Now we're getting more in line with safety where the clothing is protecting you more. On January fourth when we go to the bunker gear, that will be a tremendous thing. I think there will be a lot of pitfalls with it, but overall I think it's good. It's going to get the guys protection.

Haran: At that time the city didn't supply your own turnout gear. You had to buy your own. We had leather helmets back then. We didn't have the equipment we have today with this Nomex. We had practically raincoats, black rubber raincoats. Gloves were non-existent. They didn't issue you gloves. There was no standard for gloves. Guys were wearing leather gloves. Who was wearing rubber gloves? Everybody wore something

50

different. Then you had the boots that came up over your thighs. I was making about eighty-two dollars a week. I think I spent about a hundred and twenty dollars for a turnout coat, a helmet, and boots.

I was going to go pick up my equipment the day after I went to introduce myself at the firehouse. There was a place in Clifton called Cairns. We went up there. The fellows I came on with, we all met up there and we all bought boots and coats. I didn't know what to buy at that time. You had your option to wear either a rubber coat or a canvas coat. I was talking to the fellows there in Salvage and told them I was leaving to buy my equipment. They said, "You know you can either get a black rubber coat or you can get a canvas coat. The option is yours, but we recommend a canvas coat for you. They're much warmer than the rubber coats and you do a lot of running here. So if you're going to be here any length of time, you're better off getting a canvas coat because they're a lot warmer." So, that's what I did. We went up to Cairns. I bought a canvas coat.

At that particular time the thing was, if you're in an engine company, you got the rubber coat. If you were in a truck company, most of those guys had the canvas coats. That's what we did. The truck guys bought the canvas coats and the engine guys bought the rubber coats. I bought a canvas coat because of Salvage and the guys' recommendation. I wasn't sorry that I did that because when I went to Salvage, we did a lot of running back then. Cahill: You had your rubber coat or you had your canvas coat. It was an option. Helmets changed from the leather, which I thought was a shame. The first change was the helmets, from the leather to the plastic. Everything else stayed the same until OSHA got involved with the turnout gear. In the last five years, there were big changes in PEOSHA rules and regulations.

Highsmith: You had your choice of rubber coats and canvas coats and the difference between the two was canvas coats breathe and the rubber coats, you sweat to death. You had a choice. You could wear a long one, down to your ankles. You could wear a short one, up to your knees. You could wear whatever. In those days, I bought one of the most expensive coats, which is hanging in my garage along with my helmet dry rotting right now. It was called the duct coat and I was one of the first guys who had the yellow strip around the coat that's illuminated at night. And it had a liner in there. The liner's for the wintertime. In the summer time you take the liner out and the coat breathed. It kept nice and cool. You could work with it and it's more or less similar to the coats they wear now. I think the coats they wear now might have a little bit more rubber or something in them now.

I used to go down to Levy's in Elizabeth for the boots, seven dollars and fifty cents for a pair of steel tip boots. Our helmets were custom made. Everybody had to have their heads measured at Cairns. They were the only ones who made helmets for us. They would come down. They'd size you up and they'd make you a helmet from the size they took. There was really no rule on what kind gloves to wear like there is today.

Now OSHA makes you wear a certain type of glove, certain type of helmet, everything else. In those days you ran free, but you protected yourself. You did your best. You wouldn't go and buy something that wouldn't protect you because it's protective gear. That's why I bought the most expensive coat that I could buy and my first pair of boots was the most expensive pair of boots I could buy. I found that they were the same as the seven dollars and fifty cents boots down Levy's, exactly the same, except the ones in Levy's had a flaw in them, which you couldn't tell. Like I said, the uniform was khaki and blue shirts and black shoes.

52

The only problem about the helmet was, since they were leather, they would lose their shape if you got to enough heat. So, you knew the guys who worked in Twenty Engine, Six Engine, Ten Engine, all the companies upon the hill, their helmets were all turned, topsy-turvy, and bent in the front and the back because they went in the heat. And then some guys, they took their helmets and put them by the fire, so it would curl up, so they looked like they were in some heat.

Butler: I went right up to Universal Fire Equipment on Stuyvesant Avenue in Vailsburg. They had all the turnout gear there, which at that time you purchased yourself. You went in and he did have everything that I needed, except the helmet. I lugged it in with me when I walked into the firehouse.

You had a leather helmet with no adjustable strap or anything. The leather helmet was actually made to your head. They had a device which they stuck on your head which looked like long skinny prongs and fit it to your head. They'd punch out the fitting on the top of this machine. If you had a little bump or something, a little indentation on your head, you helmet was made like that. No chinstrap or anything with it. No eye goggles or eye protection or anything like that.

You had a rubber raincoat, just an un-insulated rubber raincoat. And a pair of firefighter boots which is one of the few things that may be improved on, but pretty much has been stable all along. Gloves you had were a pair of rubber coated gloves. The popular brand for many years was called Fireball. Just an orange glove, a little cotton lining in it, and that's the glove you used for firefighting.

Cody: I remember walking into the firehouse for the first time and the captain saying, "Find a helmet that fits you." because we didn't have our own stuff. We had our own coats but we didn't have helmets. We had gotten the coats in the Academy. He said, "Just find a helmet that fits you and ride on the back step." He showed me where to stand. I wasn't in the firehouse twenty minutes. We had a run to the projects, at the Columbus Homes. I was assigned to Four Engine. I remember coming back. When I came back, I found out that I had a captain's helmet on. Not knowing that the white in it was captain, but that's the one that fit me.

Garrity: We had leather helmets. We had two types of coats, one was canvas and one was rubber, a Midwestern rubber coat, which was the standard. Everybody all over the country wore black rubber and they put yellow stripes on it after a while. The gloves were whatever you had. A lot of times you didn't wear gloves. Especially in the summer time, you didn't wear gloves. They weren't required. Nobody wore them which meant you had a lot of punctures, a lot of scratches, cuts, and burns on your hand. But it wasn't until things changed where protection became more important that you wore gloves.

I don't think I had a pair of gloves the first summer I worked. Then we started to get those black rubber gloves, the neoprene gloves. Some guys had those. Someone gave me a pair of woolen mittens. They were just big heavy woolen mittens. I wore those for a couple of years. Then we started to buy leather gloves after a while. After you get burnt or cut enough you figure, "Well, maybe I should do something." I started to wear gloves.

If you happened to be in the hardware store, you'd pick up a pair of leather gloves, the cowhide gloves. I think they were five dollars. You'd buy a pair of those until they wore out or they shrank because you dried them on the radiator and tried to get your hands in them. You looked like you had a hook on the end of your arm. The boots were the same boots we have today. The only difference was they didn't have a steel shank. It was the same style boot.

Equipment wise, the only thing that's changed is it's now rubber coated Nomex instead of rubber coated canvas, the plastic helmets, and now those gloves that they wear. Everything else is basically the same design, the same colors. So, it's still the same fire department as far as the clothing looks. I like the helmet we wear. I like that style of helmet compared to the other ones. I know guys who wear that metropolitan type helmet and they tell me you get burns on the back of your neck. Where the helmet we wear, at least it covers the back of your neck. It may be traditional, but it's functional.

As a matter of fact, I wore one of those helmets when I was on the safety committee. They gave us some of these things to test. I tested the ones we wear now and I tested the metro. I didn't like the metro. It was too short. Didn't fit right, had to wear a chinstrap with it which I don't like. Because when you're wearing a chinstrap and you have to put your mask on, the chinstrap's in the way. That's just personal preferences.

The leather helmets were made to fit your head. When you bought a leather helmet, you went up to Cairn's and they put a thing on you head and made a mold. The inner mold of the helmet fit your head. So you could put it on your head. Shake your head; stand upside down; it wouldn't come off. I still have it. Doesn't fit anymore because it shrank, but I still have it.

McGovern: You had to buy your coat. They told me. They gave me a week to buy a coat. That was the old rubber raincoat that we had to buy. We had to burn the lining to get the lint off it. That was the first thing you did with the old coats. You'd lay it on the table and light it. All the lint would burn off it. That was a common procedure back then. The idea was when you went out in a fire it doesn't burn while you're in it. The inside was a felt liner, but it had like a light fuzz all over it. You had to burn that off. Otherwise while you were wearing it, it would go right up through you.

The helmets were the old leather, custom fit helmet, which I still have. Gloves were the rubber Fireball, the old rubber Fireball that they banned. They used to get stiff as a board after a couple of uses and they melted every time you touched a hot box spring. Boots were the thigh length pull up. I think they were Service. You put in a leather coated metal shank. That was bought separately. The boots didn't come with it.

Pianka: At the time we had the old McIntosh type coats. That was just an overcoat, essentially a rubber raincoat, the three quarter boats, a leather helmet and regular gloves, construction type rubber gloves. There wasn't a great emphasis on protective gear. As a matter of fact, some of the stuff I was getting was hand me downs. Then I looked at some of the old timers. They were wearing the old canvas coats yet. I mean it was really crazy. There was no protection. They had holes in them to boot.

But right after that things started changing, in the '70s. I think that's when the safety aspect starting coming. Little by little other things came into being like the change of turnout gear, the plastic helmets, stuff like that. I don't know if it made that much of a difference on a day-to-day basis because some of the safety gear is fine, but it's also detrimental. The guys

56

complained about the mask being heavy. Well it is heavy. You have to work harder. The new gear we have is harder to work in, but it gives you more protection, and it's great in the winter. I think it's a tradeoff, I guess as far as gear goes.

McDonnell: We had a rubber coat and the rubber boots. The boots didn't all have steel shanks. You could have gotten the steel shank or you could get inserts. You could get leather inserts for the nails. That's what I had. Pretty much, that's what everybody had because guys didn't like the steel shank. They claimed they made your feet cold in the winter. When you bought the boot, they would make a leather insert that you put in the boot. They wore out. You used to wear holes in them. After a while I used to buy two and double them up. When they would get old and you would take them out, you could see the holes in the bottom, the nails. They were worn almost all the way through. We didn't have a steel toe that I remember. No gloves. We didn't wear gloves. We didn't have to. You bought gloves if you wanted gloves, whatever kind you wanted. Most guys probably in those days didn't wear gloves. They couldn't work with them.

Melodic: We had a leather helmet, which I wish I still had. I'd give a million bucks for that, but where it's at God only knows. Had that, I had like a raincoat, a pair of rubber gloves, and then we had a totally different type of mask than what we use today. Which was light and nice, but in the long run they weren't good. So, they did away with them. What else, boots, no bunker gear, just a long coat like a rain coat, long pair of boots, gloves, and a helmet and that was that. The boots had metal shanks in them.

57

Believe it or not that I preferred the old turnout gear. You were able to move around much easier and it wasn't as hot as what we have today.

Rotonda: The turnout gear was the high boots, the leather helmet, and the rubber coats. And another thing I learned, long sleeve shirts certainly help also. Me and Bobby Linsey were standing side by side at a job. The heat was so bad. We couldn't go anywhere. We were like stuck together. We had a line and we're up against the garage door. We turned the helmets around backwards to keep the heat off our faces and everything.

When the ordeal was over and we finally got the fire knocked down a little bit, he had burns on his arms right through the coat. He had first degree burns and I had nothing. The only thing is I had a long sleeve shirt. I never would wear short sleeve shirts for that reason. Now we have this other stuff. You're in trouble with all this gear you put on. You can hardly even work at a fire. You just die. On a hot day before you even move you're ready to lie down and take a rest. Because you start sweating so bad when there's real hot weather. No way. This will kill you. This equipment you're wearing now.

T. Grehl: Long, down to about your knees rubber coats. The old pull up boots that went up to your thighs. So you were basically covered well for any water. Rubber Fireball gloves, orange and a fitted helmet that was customized to your head. It was a leather helmet that they actually molded the inside to fit your head exactly perfect.

Ryan: I had a leather helmet, rubber raincoat and as it would get torn it was touched promptly with duct tape. Some of the people looked rather silver after a while there was so much duct tape on their coat. But they got the job done. That evolved rapidly. The leather helmet we were only able to wear that for a couple of years. Then we went to the first plastic helmet. Next change we got Globe coats, which were better insulated, getting us away from the raincoats. Unfortunately, they weren't waterproof and you would get soaked. Everything was constantly wet.

We had the rubber Fireball gloves which stunk. You'd go into any given firehouse and there'd be a rack of driers on top of radiators and people's gloves would be drying out. The stench was very peculiar to rubber Fireball gloves. Probably the most dramatic change was going to the bunker pants, the bunker gear outfits. It's encapsulated the people. It helps and it hinders. So, I suppose it's a trade off. Everybody was wearing gloves. If you didn't, you got burnt. Everybody wore these old stupid Fireball gloves.

Langenbach: We had the Nomex coat. I had to buy a Nomex coat. We still had the leather helmets. Then we changed to the polycarbonate helmet. Then you could buy the rubberized Nomex. I think Midwestern made a coat that kept you a little drier. And then we went to this new crap. I don't think the new guys appreciate that we had to buy everything ourselves. It wasn't given to us.

So, you had to buy a helmet. In the beginning it was a leather helmet. You bought it in one place. There was another place you could buy boots, Jackson's. But anyway, you'd buy a helmet. It was a Nomex coat. We had just gone to Nomex from the canvas, so it was a Nomex coat and the full-length boots. Of course, you had to buy all the other stuff, your dress uniform and your work clothes, all that other stuff. That was all the polyester then. The first big change was the helmets went from leather to polycarbonate. Leather was out; polycarbonate is in.

The leather helmet cost you quite a bit because it was sized to your head. That's one thing. It wasn't adjustable. The polycarbonate was adjustable. Everybody loved their leather helmets. They had their own character. You could bend them and twist them and they get wet. Well, you see guys still have leather helmets. It was very comfortable.

The polycarbonate was, of course like anything else new, a piece of shit. What do I need this for? Somebody's making money off us because you had to go back to Universal Fire Equipment. Who owned Universal? We had to go back there. Now you had to order that, to buy that. And then we went to the Midwestern coat. The Nomex coat was good except you got soaking wet. Everybody got wet. So then Midwestern came out with a rubberized Nomex. That was a little bit heavier, but you stayed drier. Some of the truck guys had longer coats. They had a truck length coat. Then we went to this new thing we have now with the short coat and the turnout pants.

With the gloves you could always tell who wore them. A guy who wore gloves always had burns on his wrists because he would always stick his hands out. His coat would stop here; his gloves would stop here; and you would get burned here. The guys who didn't wear gloves had burns all over his hands, but he was more like a turtle. He'd pull himself back in. We bought our own. Then the popular glove to have was the Fireball, the orange Fireball. It was like five bucks a pair. They lasted a pretty long time. They were warm. They kept your hands dry, but they melted. You'd touch something too hot and the gloves would melt. You could see the guys who had done something stupid because the inside of the glove was all melted. But they were almost like throwaways.

We had the glove driers. I think every firehouse has their own concocted glove drier sitting on top of the steam radiator to dry your gloves. At that time I don't think there was any standard because everybody wore what they wanted to. A lot of guys in the trucks wore the leather workman's gloves or even the cowhide gloves, but there was no real standard. You'd see a guy who never wore gloves. He was a hell of an engine man. But he never wore gloves. It was the half macho, the half "This is what we always did. We're not changing."

I didn't really deal with the fully encapsulated turnout gear, just the tail end and it was just a little bit out roving. It's going back to the old, maybe being a dinosaur. When I came on the job, it was the perfect time to come on the job to be a fireman. It was the perfect time to be a fireman who was going to be a boss later on because we went to fire after fire after fire. You knew what worked and what didn't work. And you knew how to behave in a fire. You knew what to half way expect what a fire was doing.

Well, now we've taken the new guy, he's never going to see the fires that we saw. He's never going to get that experience of going to fire after fire. We've taken him and we've fully encapsulated him, so he's isolated from the environment around him so he has no idea what the environment is really like. We knew as firemen with the old stuff, that when your ears got too hot, you got lower. If you didn't get lower and you kept putting water on it, but it still got hot, well something wasn't right. We have to back out of here and figure out what the hell we're doing wrong.

The new kid doesn't know that. He doesn't know it because he never did it before. There's nothing we can do anywhere to teach him what this is going to be like. And then we wrap him up in this cocoon and say, "Okay, go in there and put out the fire." He thinks he's superman. We're going to get kids killed. I'm glad it hasn't happened, but I see in the future, we're going to get people hurt.

We all know, anybody who is a student of this job knows that heart attacks and strokes kill more firefighters than anything else. More of us go down from heart attacks and strokes than burning buildings and collisions, whatever. So, now we've taken the kid, we have no plan to maintain his physical capabilities through his career. You're through the door and twenty-five years later, we'll see you later. Have a nice life. So, we've taken this guy now and we've put him in this cocoon again where his body core temperature goes up to who knows what. We run him like a maniac the one or two fires he's going to get a month and we're going to get people hurt that way, too.

Long term, we're going to see a lot of stress on the guys. So, are they safer? Yes, they're safer. Are they better off? Maybe they're not better off. I don't know. And I don't know what the future holds. We keep regulating ourselves away from whatever, away from doing our job. Again it's not a bad thing. I don't want to see guys get hurt. Just to say, "I'm a fireman. I'm supposed to get burned because I'm a fireman." That's nonsense. But we're setting people up to get hurt. I think they're being set up. And well-intentioned people who don't really have a grasp on what it is a fireman does are setting standards for us that we're stuck with. We're forced to live with. I mean OSHA looks at a fireman's job the way they look at an electrician's job or anything else. "Here's the hazard. To avoid the hazard you do this. We'll either take the hazard away or if we can't do that, then we'll protect you in such a way that you'll never get hurt." Well, they don't think there's something in between there.

We still expect the fireman to go into a building and put fires out. We don't expect him to stand out on the street and put the fire out. If there's somebody inside the building, we expect him to go inside and get the person out of the building. So, now we're making it so this kid is going to get himself hurt and again going back to what I said originally about the time I came on the job. All those bosses or leaders or supervisors of my generation are almost all gone or they're slowly going little by little. When they're gone that knowledge base is going to go with them. Now the new captain, the firemen who never went to fires is now becoming the captain who never went to fires, is going to be a Battalion Chief, a Deputy Chief and whatever else. Now he's leading people who are less experienced than him. I don't know. I don't know what the answer is. I don't think there is an answer. But I'm just saying it. I'm throwing that out as a comment. It's kind of scary.

Luxton: We were the first ones with the plastic helmets, the New Yorkers, us and the cadets, Gerry Rosamilia and Harry Kapinowski, Kevin Burkhardt, Bruce Morgan, Gerry Lardiere. They were the cadets. They had them and we had them. I think that was a pre-requisite. You had to have your uniform. Now I was fortunate because I had Nutley uniforms and Newark called for the Big Yanks. They didn't have the khaki and gray anymore. They had gone to the blues. And I had line uniforms in Nutley. I remember it was a big coupe that I was able to use my Nutley uniforms. So I saved some money there. You had to buy the boots and a rubber coat.

You had the old rubber coat and the new helmets and, of course, the Fireball gloves. We had the Fireball gloves.

Connell: We were the first required to buy the new NFPA specs turnout coats and stuff. The first one I bought was an A. L. B. It wasn't water resistant. Every time you went to a fire, you came back drenched. About three or four years later, all the seams and everything started dry rotting out of it. It was supposedly a Nomex coat, but at that time the liners could be taken out and they usually were during the summer time. They really didn't have that much heat protection to it and it did leak like a sieve. It was poorly made and everything was dry rotting on it. The boots were three quarter length, steel toe and shank. Helmet is polycarbonate and the gloves are Fireballs.

There's been a tremendous change in the turnout gear. I'm not in the field, so I'm not dealing with it every day, but I do wear it when we train. It's great during the winters, but it's completely overrated. The amount of burns firemen suffer, if anything, went up a little bit more with the new turnout gear due to compression burns because your sweat turns to steam inside your gear in a fire. In the summer it makes you overheated. It's a little harder to work with and in my opinion the old way was a better way. The hoods are great during the winter, but only to keep you warm. Like everybody else, I guess, if I was in the field I'd still have my hood in my pocket except for the winter times during outside operations.

Pignato: We had to buy our own Nomex coats. The insides quickly rotted away. All you had was the Nomex shell on the outside. I should have kept one of those darn things. Most guys were wearing these coats for years with

64

the quilted liner inside between you and the Nomex. That was the only fire protection you had. That's what we wore because the liner used to rot away. You would end up just throwing the stuff away. Those coats were expensive.

We had to buy our own out of our clothing allowance. I never cheated myself. I had a couple of coats. I bought turnout pants and I used to buy boots all the time. If they leak, I'm buying new ones. When I climb on the roof, I want traction. The metal shanks weren't really required. Guys were still buying these stupid bulletproof material things that they used to stick on the board with thumbtacks. They were all sold a bill of goods at one time to buy these inserts for their boots. I was told there was a department order. They had to buy these things. Somebody got rich and they really didn't work. Stuff came right through them. It was a bulletproof material and nails still came through. You had a few nails poke into your skin all the time.

You could use any gloves you wanted. I preferred leather gloves and the Fireballs. The Fireballs weren't as cold. I also wore mittens for the wintertime. I used the Fireballs if I got detailed to the engine. Most of the time I'd wear leather gloves. Never had a problem with them; never got burnt through them. They worked better. I could feel what I was doing. The gloves today, they just don't feel right.

Langevin: Turnout gear was rubber hip boots, canvas coat that came down just above the knee, plastic helmets and rubber gloves, big monstrosity orange things. We had just changed to plastic helmets. Safety wasn't too well thought of. I think they expected you to get the job done no matter what it took.

Perdon: It was like a raincoat almost. We were given the Civil Defense coats until we got our own. We had to buy our own stuff; you had something with a liner in it then. The liner came in and out for summer and wintertime. It was a thin liner and then actually in the summer you were in like a raincoat. There was nothing in between. It was only to shed the water. There was no protection from the heat. But it was one of those things again. That was life. You lived with it. Not until you came with all this other shit did you realize there's a better way.

The helmet was typical of what it is now. It wasn't the leather. I didn't have the leather. I bought the new issue and that was it. That's what I always had. I never went leather. The boots were three quarter boots with steel shank. Gloves, you could just start using anything. Sometimes guys didn't use them. You had the Fireballs, but they were too ugly looking. I swear to God. You had guys getting leather gloves, but then once they got wet they were useless. So, now you experiment with different things and you always came back to the Fireballs. That was probably the best. But there were a lot of guys who at that time didn't wear gloves. It was like if you didn't wear them there wasn't anybody there to tell you, to say wear gloves.

We switched over to the heavier coats; it had to be in the '80s. At Seventeen Engine we were just wearing the rubber coat with the liner that you could take in and out. Six Engine when I first got there, we still had the removable liner. It had to be the late '80s that you finally went to where you couldn't take the liner out. That's when they did all the inspecting. You couldn't even have a little hole in it. I mean I wore coats where they were just ripped. That was okay.

Bisogna: Three quarter length coat, rubber boots, the coat wasn't rubber, but it wasn't Nomex either. It was whatever that blend was, kind of a canvas. It usually worked well. It kept you dry and pretty warm in the winter. The only drawback was sometimes you were cold in the wintertime and wet. Boots didn't give you that much weather protection. But if it was in the twenties, I put long johns on and I was usually fine. The only time you really got cold was when you're standing around after the job was over. Then your muscles started getting tight. Then you got cold because you were wet and there was no flame and you're not working. So, that was hardest part.

I liked that gear better than the gear we have now only because in the summertime this stuff is going to kill somebody. It's just so hot. You can't put it on in the weather that's ninety, hazy, hot, and humid. You put it on. You're sweating. You sweat right through your pants. I'm not in the shape I was in then either. So, you worry about heat exhaustion more. Somebody's going to pay for this stuff eventually. But anyway, they say it's safer. I'm not going to knock the system. In my opinion, it's probably one of the worst things because it doesn't repel the water. Water comes off the ceiling, hits you in the shoulder and two seconds later it's on your skin. It goes right through that coat. Then the coat weighs fifty pounds. If you put it on the floor, you have a hard time picking it up.

As far as fire protection, hey, I'll take your word for it, but to tell you the truth, I never got that close where I needed to have that much protection. If you're that close to a fire, it's time to back up. Let's be real, it's not an entry suit. So, the other stuff in the summertime you could leave your boots down until you got a little wet, but at least you didn't have twenty minutes and you're ready to die. You felt you could work for a while. But the new stuff is tough, tough on me anyway. I think a lot of guys probably feel the same way. What can you do? They give it to you. That's a nice deal. We had to buy the coat, the hip boots and your helmet.

The helmet was a plastic helmet. They weren't leather. It was the New York model. I think it might have coast fifty bucks, forty, forty to fifty dollars I think it was. It wasn't a lot of money. Now they're a couple of hundred, I guess. I don't even know because they give it to you. The coat was the most expensive. That might have been a hundred and fifty, sixty dollars, something like that. And the boots were thirty, forty. They weren't a lot of money. Then again, we weren't making a lot of money. I think money has devalued over the years, too.

The only thing they gave you was a pair of sheets and a pillowcase with your badge number stamped on it. And they made a big production out of that. The joke was everybody liked this because here you are getting on the job and they're giving you sheets and a pillowcase with your badge stamped on. I thought that was pretty neat. That was the only thing they gave you. Welcome to the fire department. Here's a pillowcase. All right, thanks a lot. This job can't be too bad.

I wore gloves. We had Fireballs. You had to buy them yourself. They were like a rubber glove. They were good as far as abrasions, but not a lot of heat. They were decent, had some feel with them anyway. The new ones we have now, there's so much insulation on them you can't feel anything. Again, they get soaked. The Fireballs got a little wet inside and after several wettings they stank. You had to get new ones because your hands would smell after a while if you put on the old pair. But I thought they worked well. I never got cut with one of them on. I guess if you really ran across a sharp edge it would go through it, but they were pretty good protection.

Ricca: It had just changed from the leather helmets to the plastic helmets right around that time. I had a plastic helmet. The guys with the leather helmets looked at the thing like it was strange or poked at it like it was an animal in a cage, wondering what the heck it was. Back then you had to buy your own stuff, everything came out of pocket.

We had the first Cairns plastic helmet, without the donut in it. Fireball gloves, everybody had. Nomex, we were probably one of the first groups to have Nomex. When Nomex got wet, especially being heavy before, once they got wet or you sweated, the thing was a million pounds. Either my brother Angelo or my brother Joe gave me a coat, an old rubber coat, and I liked it a lot more. The old timers still wore the rubber; some of the guys wore the rubber coats without the stripes on them. That's how old some of the coats were.

The pull up boots, Ranger was the big name. I remember that. You made bunker pants out of an old pair of blue jeans, old pair of bell bottoms. You'd put them over the boots and that's what they called the night rig at that time. You'd wear jeans, a lot of guys, not everybody, a lot of guys would wear jeans over their boots the way we're wearing the bunker pants today. And in the winter, the jeans were a lot warmer for you.

Since I've been a captain, the turnout gear is obviously much different than it was when I first came on the job. You could pull the liner out back then, which I think nine out of ten guys did. The Fireball gloves I was happy to see go. I burned my hands on many occasions with those gloves. One particular incident, we were on Elizabeth Avenue, Ray Stoffers and myself, and the boom of the ladder pipe from I guess it was Nine Truck started hitting us. We're behind a chimney and Ray's yelling, "Shut that thing off." And I said, "Ray, I don't think they can hear us." So, we started throwing stuff off the roof. We were around where the roof was pretty well heated. We're throwing flashing and it's burning us because the gloves are melting to our fingers. But we're just trying to stop getting hit from the ladder pipe. To see the new gloves come in, I thought that was a good advantage.

But the bunker gear for myself, it's a misery. It's too hot. The hood, forget about it. The hood, I think is putting somebody in a place to get cooked. Because when your ears feel like they're getting pinched with pliers, time to go out. Your ears just tell everything. Even when you're ventilating, the roof's open. You feel that rush of air coming behind you. I just don't care for the hood at all. You wear it because it's mandatory. I felt a lot more mobile with the other coat and the pull up boots, a lot more comfortable. But then again that's after wearing it for so long. A new guy coming on the job gets used to the bunker gear the way it is now and probably feels more protected.

Are they over protecting us? I think we've had stuff jammed down our throats without us saying what we wanted. Not by the city, but mandated through PEOSHA or whoever makes the laws. Sometimes I think there isn't a firefighter that has anything to say about it that sits on the board or whoever makes the decisions. Or they're asking some guy from Burlington or Hunterdon County his input. You can't, you've got to ask guys from the inner parts of the city who are going to fires. Nobody ever had a poll. Even when we get tested putting it out in the field. They give it to you as a test and then nobody ever comes back to say "How was it?" If it was good, it doesn't matter anyway because the decisions made that it's not good for you. And everybody is, "Well, big brother I guess."

Gesualdo: Turnout gear, rubber coats just below the knee, hip boots with steel plates, toe caps, gloves at the time were Fireballs, which was kind of a rubber covered canvas or cotton, polycarbonate helmets with cold weather flaps and eye protection. That was pretty much it with personal gear, which we purchased on our own, replaced on our own, as well as the work clothes, work jacket, and the dress uniform. Everything was purchased by us.

Chapter Four: Masks

Fredette: We had those little canister masks. We had them, but they were always under the driver's seat. The hose on them was always flattened out from the weight of the mask. Nobody ever checked the dates of the canister. I never remember any of the firemen ever using a mask. That changed after the war.

Vetrini: Well, we had the masks and eventually it was an order, you had to have the mask hooked on to you. Normally, we would get to a fire, you would operate, and if you needed a mask somebody would go out and get a mask. After about two years it was standard operating procedure that you had the mask on all the time, but they were the MSA all service masks, the Burrells. After we left training, they started to more or less set a procedure with masks. But the old timers were gung-ho. They didn't bother with the mask. Then we came with the self-contained, then later on with the Scott air packs. The very beginning there was very little. I don't recall that we had to take a mask in all the time.

Redden: We didn't have masks in Two Engine. We had them in Sixteen. I think when I got promoted from Two Engine in '54 I guess it was, we started getting the filter type masks. But when I came on the job the mask people were in the Squad. They had the Chemox mask, the Navy mask. They were the mask people. Some of the Trucks might have had filter type masks.

Kinnear: There were masks on the engines, but they weren't used at all. You couldn't really do a close approach like you do today. You stayed back. With a two and a half inch line you could stay back because you had a lot of reach with it. Basically, you drowned them. If it was a one room job, you'd do it the same as you do today. It would take you a little longer to work your way into the room naturally, but you did it. Of course, you had more men, too. So the guy on the tip would go as far as he could. Then there would be another fresh man to relieve him. You'd just work your way into it. You took a lot of smoke, but nobody knew any different. You took it and that was it. It was part of the job.

We had two types of masks. We had the all service and we had the Chemox, but they stayed in the boxes. We never used them. I don't remember when we really first started using them. Probably in the early '50s and then we almost exclusively used the all-service masks. Except for drills we hardly ever took the Chemox off the rig. We used it at drills, but I don't think I ever put one on at a fire. I wore the filter mask, the all-service mask, all the time and I never really had any problem with it. I had to bail out twice. One time we were trying to get into a cellar, which was foolish, and a second time was shortly before I made captain at a fire on Bergen Street. The fire was in the third floor and the cockloft. I was the first man up, opened a fog nozzle and everything came back down. I started to feel woozy. What had happened was I had knelt down and had crimped the hose, so I wasn't getting anything. That wasn't the mask's fault. Eddy Vesey grabbed me, took me into a room, and broke a window.

I loved the all-service mask. You could put them on while you were going to the fire. All the guys had them on when you got there. You didn't have to start putting the straps on like you do today. You had to be careful.

You couldn't go into a cellar or an area where the oxygen was deficient. They sat on the front of your chest. It was easy to put on. It was light and I had good results with it. Of course, with the changes and everything, I'm sure it's better they went to the air mask.

Masters: Masks? We had a shoe store go on Orange Street across from Saint Rose of Lima. I forget the side street. The side street went up against the railroad. So, we had the MSA masks. You know the little red containers. They weren't worth shit. So, we go in the basement and it's smoky. Now, from what I read, that mask was operable if you had sixteen percent oxygen in the basement. The smoke was down to the floor. We stayed there. We overhauled, knocked the ceiling down. So, we start going up the basement stairs. I see guys dropping to the ground. After that I don't remember. I wake up and I'm lying on the ground, too. They were giving us oxygen. That's how good our mask was.

That was quite a while before they changed to the SCBAs. But I remember, we wore the MSAs and the Chemox. I remember they had the breathing bag in front. It attached from the front. But you had to have somebody help you put it on. We didn't use them too much. They were cumbersome.

F. Grehl: The men on the Rescue Squad were the mask specialists except for companies like Twelve Engine, Six Engine, Seven Engine, Twenty Engine, Ten Engine. They wouldn't give the line to the Rescue Squad. I wasn't on the fire department that long before I went to Six Engine where things were changing.

When we first went on the job, we had all service masks. You could use them under almost all conditions except for below grade firefighting where the oxygen content was depleted or anywhere else where the oxygen content was depleted. When I went on the job they were in boxes, each had its own box. There were either three or four of them that were put in a bigger box with a canvas cover on it up on top of the apparatus. When I got to Six Engine, our Battalion Chief was Donlon, who came from the Rescue Squad. He was very, very versed on masks from the Rescue Squad. Donlon is starting to change things. He started training the whole Fourth Battalion on use of masks.

Of course, when I went to Six Engine, we had the masks. Not only did we have them, we took them out of the boxes and we hung them on the ladder, on the back, on the suction hose, on each side, or hung them up over on the bar on the top, so that when we were going to a fire, we put them on. When we jumped off the rig we had the masks on and we were ready to go. That was one of Donlon's innovations. We had our own masks.

We had Teddy Smith, who never wore a mask in his life. "I wouldn't put on a gook-gook." He used to call them gook-gooks. "I don't put no gook-gook on." But, he was right there. I don't care how thick the smoke was, he stood right with you. One time I had a nozzle and we were working our way down a hallway. We get into a room and the thing was hot. It started coming back. I said to Teddy, "Teddy come on, we have to back out into the hallway. It's too damn hot in here." "I'm all right kid. I'm all right kid. I stay with you. Don't worry. I won't leave you." I said, "Teddy back up. We're going back to the hallway." "I'm all right kid." I have to push him. In pushing him we end up rolling out in the hall. Just about that time the fire comes out over our heads out into the hall. I'm lying on the floor with the hose line trying to push it back in. The captain comes up and says,

"What the hell are you two guys doing?" I said, "We're all right, cap." But Teddy said, "I stay with you kid, I stay with you." He did.

All this was happening when I went to Six Engine. Around 1950, I guess it was, when he got promoted to Battalion Chief. That's when it happened. Donlon and Crowley and Donahue, they were the three captains in the Squad when they really started using masks. We got that training from Donlon. And I think Crowley probably did it on his tour. They worked together, very well together on opposite tours. That's when we started to put the masks on, took them out of the boxes and started to use them.

Vesey: We were using Burrells, canister type. They had that and the trucks carried them. They had the Chemox, but they weren't used too often. They were a little too cumbersome. They weren't anything like the Burrells. The Burrells you could throw them on. They were smaller and wider. The Chemox were for certain conditions, last resorts. Never saw too many people wear them either. In fact, a lot of guys didn't know where the hell they were. Yes, the guys who wore masks. They liked them.

The only thing I could find wrong with them was when they didn't change the canister. Somebody would use it at the change of shifts or even during the day. A guy would use one or maybe forget to change the canister. They had a piece of tape on the bottom and were just chemically filtered. A lot of guys liked them. They were small, snap on, snap off. That's all the Squad used. Sometimes they got too careless with them. Used them in spots they shouldn't have. They figured it was bomb proof.

I never liked the mask. I used it a couple of times. You'd walk around banging on doors, walking into walls. Suppose you go down the cellar or something like that? I've done that without a mask. Stayed down low and gave it a shot. If it was too ripe, I'd let the guys with the masks go in. I'll crack a window for you and take doors out.

McCormack: We had Burrell canister masks, which were rarely if ever used. They were Mine Safety Appliance tools that were primarily for work in mines, not for the fire service. But that's all there was at the time. No one used them. I mean we were taught to use them, but it wasn't the accepted practice.

I once had an old time Chief ball me out for putting a mask on. I can't blame the man. That was the prevailing custom at the time. I was a fresh kid, I guess, and I saw an opportunity. I had been doing a little studying and saw a fire where I thought, "This would be a perfect opportunity to put a mask on." So I put the mask on and was walking down the street expecting to put the face piece on, go into the building, and do some real serious work inside the building. He caught me and said, "Where are you going?" I said, "I'm going to go in with such and such company." He said, "Take that mask off kid. If you're going to be a fireman, you better learn how to take a belly full of smoke."

The masks were placed on top of the apparatus in boxes. Every apparatus had a box on top, a gray box with five Burrell masks inside. Each mask was in a little red box made out of some kind of composition board. It was red with black metal trimming on it. Latches on the front to keep it locked and the mask was usually folded inside of that. It was taken out periodically and checked, looked over, but as far as operating with them at fires, they were rarely, rarely if ever used. Nothing like what you have today.

We had fewer fires. When I was a young fireman, I didn't go to nearly as many fires as the young firemen go to today. But I didn't have the protection they have either. I didn't have the Scott air-pack mask and I didn't have inch and three quarter line. If we had a good mattress fire or a bedroom fire, you would go into this place and take a tremendous beating. You'd be in there working for whatever it was, ten minutes, fifteen minutes sucking in that raw smoke and taking it. Very often you would throw-up, vomit. You'd stagger out of the building heaving and coughing and choking. It wasn't a pleasant situation.

So we only did that a few times a year compared to these young kids today who do it every day they're working. They may be actually taking less of a beating than we took in those days because of the masks they're wearing, the self-contained masks.

In my era, the masks were inefficient to start with and we wouldn't bother to wear them most of the time. It was frowned upon to wear a mask. The Rescue Squad were the mask specialists in those days. If you were in an ordinary fire company and you had a fire, you were expected to get a line into the building. To get water on the fire, which of course without a mask in a heavy smoke condition sometimes you didn't even get near the fire. You were shooting water into smoke. You couldn't get deep into the building without a mask. You did the best you could. You got the line in and tried to attack the fire, to hold on for as long as you could. When you couldn't take it anymore, you backed out of the building and someone else would take over the line for you. You held the fire until the Rescue Squad got there. They'd take over your line and put the fire out if they could.

Now with the self-contained masks you have a much more aggressive fire department, a much more efficient fire department. They go right in with their masks and their small diameter lines, go right to the seat of the fire, and get a fast knock down in a couple of minutes. It's a much more efficient operation than it was before.

Masterson: The masks were kept in a box and then you would have to take them out. By the time you got a line to work, you weren't going back to take a mask out of the box. You didn't wear them. Freddy Crowley and Jimmy Donlon made Battalion Chief. They were two squad men and they used to ride with the mask, the squad always rode with the mask. Then they had everybody in their battalion start. That's when it started, which was a good idea. We had the Burrells which were good. I still think the Burrells were good, but then they got these tanks which are a lot more weight they're putting on you to work.

Deutch: When I came on the job, Five Truck had two masks and they were both Navy type, oxygen masks. We had no all-purpose masks. We got them later on. So, you took a beating. The old timers all suffered because of that. Their lungs were affected because they didn't have those masks. In fact, I remember Johnny Fagan getting put on charges for using the Chemox , after we got a Chemox. We had a good fire in the projects, in the basement. They had about thirty Christmas trees burning. He put a Chemox on. The Chief told the captain to write him up for use of a Chemox on a fire like that. He wasn't supposed to use it because it was so expensive.

The Burrells weren't used when I went up to Five Truck in September of '54. We just had those Navy type masks, the Chemox. When the all-purpose came in, I thought they were great masks for our battalion up there with all the bedroom fires. You could taste when the canister had to be changed after about an hour of service. We had the little window. When it turned all white, then you changed them. I thought they were very good. You could have them on before you got to the fire. We always had them placed just over your head. You didn't knock yourself around like you do

79

with the tanks or get caught on the conduit. They were just in the front and out of the way. We liked them. There was no weight to them at all. But it cost the city a few dollars more than it does today. It took us a long time for everybody to get a mask, too. Then they took them off us overnight when the fireman died.

Wall: We operated with filter masks. Because Ten Truck wasn't a busy truck company, we may have had SCBAs, but I don't remember using them. Our secondary mask for confined space, ship fires, or cellar fires was the Chemox, the old N ones. The officer had to literally tell you to do that. In fact, when I first went to Ten Truck, you didn't put a mask on, even the filter mask, until the officer ordered you to put it on.

I recall our masks were under the salvage covers in boxes. So you got to a fire you had to remove the salvage cover, take out the box, and open the box with the muzzle in it, but only when the officer told you to. The officer also told you when to take the mask off. We went to the captain and said, "Look, we're all big boys. We'd like to get into the fire a little faster when we get the opportunity. Can we put the mask with our turn out gear?" Well after arguing back and forth he said, "Yes, you can, but if you ever fail to put that mask away at change of shifts, you'll never be able to do that again." So at a quarter to six, you would dutifully take your mask, pack it up, put it back in the box, and put it back in the truck. If the other tour wanted to take it out of the box, that was their problem. But I know other companies, busier companies, did respond with their masks. It was up to the captain.

Freeman: As far as masks go, you went into that macho crap. A lot of guys went in without a mask, which was crazy, but then you didn't much know about that. Some guys didn't put their mask on right away. They just went in without the mask. I would imagine eventually they would have put it on.

You can't stay in a fire building without a mask on. But initially a lot of guys didn't put their masks on. I think that was more or less macho, too. A lot of guys didn't do that.

Stoffers: The Burrells came off the rigs when I was a Battalion Chief. We got a call about three o'clock one afternoon to go around and pick up all the Burrell masks. Okay, I go and pick them all up. It seems that somebody went down into a cellar with the Burrell mask and they got killed. The widow sued and now everybody is shaking in their boots. That's when all the air tanks came in.

McGrory: Burrell masks used to be hanging on the back of the rig. They started to use them a lot more, but I don't know if we used them right.

McGee: We had the Burrell masks when I came on in '56. We thought they worked. We wore them into some pretty serious smoke conditions. Went crawling through rooms with them just like they're doing now with the self-contained breathing apparatus, but obviously they weren't as good. They were much easier to use, to put on, and they weren't heavy. So, there were some advantages to them. Unfortunately, they didn't work too well.

Denvir: We used the Burrell masks, the canister type. Some of the truck companies had Chemox masks. They didn't take them out of the box. As a matter of fact when I came on they still had the Burrells in the boxes. The busier companies were just getting around to carrying them loose on the rig where they just threw them on.

Freda: The mask that was supposed to be used when I came on the job was the MSA mask. We called them the Burrell mask. Don't ask me why. Burrell had no connection with this mask. The canister said MSA. If you asked me why they called it the Burrell, the only answer I have for you is because when I came on the job somebody said, "That's your Burrell mask." It was a canister type mask. But if you used it, you were perceived to be a sissy. The sign of a hero was the guy hanging out the window with the snot hanging out of his nose, choking, and everything. You admired him. If you went in and put your Burrell on, they would look at you and say, "Are you kidding me or what? They don't make them like they used to anymore." And you, like a nit-wit, would take your mask off not to be berated.

That changed a little bit when I went to Twelve Engine. We started to use our masks more because we just took in too much smoke on a constant basis not to. We assumed they were safe. We found out later on through a court case that they just weren't working. They weren't filtering out the toxic gases like they're supposed to be because the canisters were supposed to be kept completely dry, no moisture. When you used them the moisture from your breath would activate the main ingredient. That would convert the carbon monoxide gas into carbon dioxide.

Where did the men hang them? They were hung over the back lights of the engines and the trucks where they swung out in the weather, raining on them. Most of the time, they were totally useless. The only way you felt safe was because the noxious particles that would irritate you would be filtered out. The carbon monoxide is colorless and odorless as are some of the other gases that alarm me. When you were breathing them in you didn't even know it.

I saw a firefighter killed because of one of those masks. When I was a Squad captain, Salvatore Vacca was killed on Broad Street and one of the things that killed him was the Burrell mask. What happened was, we're inside this building and they put the Snorkel pouring straight down onto the roof, forcing all the smoke back into this building. This fellow did have his Burrell mask on and he did die from carbon monoxide poisoning. Scared the hell out of me.

Charpentier: At the time we had the Burrell. Some chiefs wanted them staying in the boxes. Others wanted you to have them out, so you put them on as you were going to a fire. Others frowned on it. It was almost like five battalions with five different procedures. Then with each tour, it was the same way. So you had almost twenty different thoughts on how to get to a fire, what to wear when you got there, and how to operate at it.

It evolved so that in normal firefighting, it was S.O.P. using a Burrell. We'd just barrel in with the Burrell on, which was good to a point. Sometimes if you bent over fighting a fire and the intake underneath was pushed up against your rubber goods, you couldn't breathe. The only time you really couldn't use one was when you had a cellar fire. Then it was up to certain companies that had the self-contained mask or the Chemox mask. A lot of guys even used them in basement fires.

Then there was an incident where a widow sued for her husband's death due to a Burrell mask. Within a matter of a couple of hours, they recalled all the Burrell masks. They were scouting all over between the truck companies, the squad, and the chiefs for the Scott self- contained or the Chemox. They were only issuing two masks to a company. Burrells were entirely out. You were put on charges if you were caught wearing one.

Our method of operating at a fire was down to nothing because out of a captain and four men you only had two masks. Either you had to stretch a line in without a mask until the other two guys masked up and took the line or you just had to stand outside. That's what you were told. Don't go in right away without the mask on. It seems our method of firefighting did a complete turnaround. It was a while before they could fill an order and give everybody at least three or four masks per company. Then we were back to aggressive firefighting again.

Smith: When they went from the Burrell to the self-contained mask, it slowed you down. When we had the Burrell, if I went into a building without a mask and it was smoky, I didn't fear too much if there was fire because that meant that it was getting enough air to support the combustion therefore I could breath. But if it was that real heavy black smoke, I used to see if I could find a window and knock it out with the inch and a half. Then put one guy with an inch and a half up along the open window on a fog to try to blow it out. With the self-contained, when it started to clear up, most men dumped the mask because it was very heavy. It was a steel tank. Most guys just dumped it.

Dunn: We started out with the filter type of mask, which worked well in the type of construction that we had in the city of Newark. When you went out of the firehouse on your fire engine you had your filter type mask on you. It's like any other tool in the fire service. You respected the mask and knew its limitations. So, the mask was with you all the time and allowed you to go quite deep into a hot fire because you never had the thought that it wasn't with you. If you started to get a taste of smoke or anything through the mask you could back out.

What happened to these masks was that, one day, Special Service units came into our firehouses and took our masks off our trucks and apparatus.

84

They said we couldn't use them anymore because there's a big legal question about the use of these masks. Several firemen across the country had been seriously injured with them. Because of that the law department in the city of Newark felt the city was in jeopardy. They took the masks off and we went into a crash program of purchasing self-contained breathing apparatus for the Newark Fire Department.

We rode without masks. What they did was, the truck companies at that time had two self-contained Scott masks. They also had some Chemox masks in reserve and on certain units in the industrial areas. They tried to re-locate them, so that every other company had something. Then as soon as they delved in and got some more almost every company was riding with two masks within 30 days. But for those other 30 days, I don't remember other companies having masks. Some units responding to the alarm had masks. The truck companies had two self-contained, but there were engine companies at that time that I can't recall having any type of protective equipment. We did go in to fight fires without masks for a short period of time.

When you make a change of that magnitude, it affected our fire fighting for a period of time because the firefighting service doesn't like change. When you took our little filter mask away and put a tank that weighs forty pounds on our backs with a limited air supply, we found when we got to the fire it was cumbersome to put on. We found numerous reasons not to use it initially, but over a period of six months the adaptation was made. You can't breathe smoke and we adapted to the new type of mask.

Extensive testing was done on the new type of mask before they were put in. I believe the first ones we bought on the Newark Fire Department were MSA's and they worked fine. Is it a better mask? They all had their place as we went through the system. I still reflect back on what we did with the filter masks and say, "Sure, in a three story frame with the windows knocked out it worked fine." Put us into a chemical company on Doremus Avenue and we probably would have killed ourselves with them. So, it was knowing the limitations of our equipment.

Carragher: When I first went to Nine Engine they had the masks in the box and they were used. You could take it out and try it on in the morning and keep it in the box right in front of you on the back of the rig right where you stood on the back step. If you had a fire, you could grab the mask and put it on. We did that. When I went to Rescue it was routine. You had a mask every morning that you set next to you. So if you were going to a fire, you put the mask right on before you even got off the truck. You got off. You were ready to go. I guess I was broken in by the time I got to Twenty Engine. Twenty Engine had the masks hanging on the back of the apparatus with the tape on the bottom so you wouldn't get the moisture. I was very conscious of masks, use of masks.

When I got promoted to captain out of Twenty Engine the members of Twenty Engine gave me my own mask, my own Burrell mask. They knew I liked the mask and I always took care of it. I used that until they took them away from us whenever it was later on in the late '60s or early '70s. But Twenty Engine used the masks. It's interesting to note certain guys you worked with would say, "Hey what are you doing with that mask on, Jerk." or something like that. All of the sudden they were over there heaving or puking their guts out. "Hey, what's the matter with you guys?" We're up in front of them with the mask on doing what you have to do. But overall I think a lot of guys liked the mask. You used them.

The Burrell mask was dangerous in a basement or something like that because you had no warning of what's going on. You were there. I think the gassings were common, more common than you realized then. But I know myself in the Rescue Squad, many times you'd come back with a headache and you'd be red. The captain would say, "Man, you're red." You wouldn't realize you were under carbon monoxide poisoning. You actually had been gassed and not realized it. But the masks were used, more in the busier companies. Guys liked them and you couldn't let somebody else get ahead of you. So if you didn't have the mask on you were going to get run over.

I loved them. They worked very well if you were above ground. The majority of fires they probably would have worked very well. It's just that when you're in a basement or where there's a lack of oxygen, now you have to be careful of it. I know a couple of guys who were overcome with the Burrells on. They got into concentrations that were too rich. There was no way of determining what the concentration was just by looking or anything like that. The Rescue Squad at the time when I first went there had a Wolf Safety Lamp. Actually it's a mine lamp. You used to light the lamp and when the lamp went out you knew you didn't have oxygen so you'd have to leave the building. But you're carrying a lantern around and who wants to carry a lantern around when you're in a fire. So we never carried it, but we had one.

It was mostly the older guys who didn't use the masks. I don't know whether they were afraid of it. In the late '40s, the Rescue Squad carried the masks and used them. Guys who came on in the late '40s didn't use the masks. They had them, but they didn't use them. The Rescue Squad guys were more proficient at using them. They used them all the time. They got used to them. They were comfortable with them. Other guys didn't use them at all, especially truck men. The truck men figured, "Who needs it? It's in the way when you're pulling the ceilings." So they tended not to use them.

It was probably in the mid-'60s to '70s when the guys really got into masks heavy. Guys then realized, "Hey, this mask is an important thing for us." It was probably the guys who came on in '59 who weren't taking the beatings that the guys who came on in the '40s were taking. Maybe the guys in '59 realized, "Hey, we have this thing. Why don't we use it?" That's when they really started. Maybe it was better training at that time that taught the older guys, "Hey, these things work." They did work.

Haran: Well, we had the old Burrell masks. It was a face piece with a tube going down into a canister about maybe half the size of a cigar box. It had all these different chemicals in it. But it turned out later that they weren't worth a damn. So we had a lot of false security there when we went into these fires. Guys back then were going into fires that I don't think guys today could have gone into without a mask or wouldn't want to. You'd be stupid to do it in retrospect. It turned out later that the masks were either no good or more than insufficient. There was some case with a huge settlement. A widow collected because her husband died.

When I was in Salvage, we had a Chemox mask, which was very large and cumbersome. You'd blow up two big lungs on your chest. We had a canister about the same size as the Burrell. It used to amaze me back then because after we used it they wanted us to seal it up and re-use it again at the next fire. I think there was a two-hour duration, depending on how rapidly you were breathing. You'd use it up. We did use them at fires. I caught a couple of ship fires. We used them in the ship fires back there. I went to two ship fires down in the port. I only can remember using them in a ship fire.

Cahill: The masks were the Burrells, the all-purpose. And we used them for years. It was so light. You just swung it over your neck as you were rolling. You wouldn't put them on in quarters necessarily, not until you got a smoke condition or something like that because you could just whip them on so quickly.

They were very difficult to breathe and work in. You had to have seventeen percent oxygen to even use it. They were no good in a cellar fire. But that was the backbone of the fire department anyway. You didn't have anything different so you didn't know. There were good points. They were light, easy to put on, easy to work with, very difficult to breathe through because if you got winded, you had a hard time breathing through them. They were functional. They functioned for a long, long time.

Some department lost a lawsuit over it. They walked into the firehouse one day, took every mask off the apparatus and walked out. So, what we had, in Salvage we had four Chemox. But they were the only masks. They were the only Chemox probably in the whole division. So we had no masks for practical purposes. That was the time between changing over from the Burrells to the self-contained masks. It had to be a month or two. They just walked in and we didn't know what the heck was going on. They started taking all the masks off, took them out.

Highsmith: The type of equipment we used was just about the same as today except that a mask that we used was just a little canister mask.

Nobody really got hurt in Newark with them. Then they started getting the air packs, but by that time I was out of the firefighting end of the business. When the Burrells got too hot, those masks didn't work. You couldn't get anything. And another thing we had, on the bottom of it, where the air used to come through and filter through the chemicals, we used to keep tape over it so moisture couldn't get in there. A lot of times you ran into a fire and you forgot to un-tape it and you couldn't breathe. I loved those MSA masks because you were fully dressed and ready to fight the fire when you got there.

We had an old Ward LaFrance with a cab. It had two compartments behind the engine driver where you could sit in. But the wagon, we had none. Very few of our apparatus had that. So you had about a two and a half to three foot platform that you had to stand on. Your mask and your clothes and everything hung back there. You would jump in your boots and dress while driving down the street. Once you got to the fire, you were fully clothed, masked, and ready to go. No one had to hook the mask up. No one had to take the tank off. You were ready to go, ready to roll. Once you got there you were ready to get inside, stop, mask up, and go forward.

Butler: You had masks. You had a little Burrell canister that was supposed to filter out any of the harmful elements through a charcoal layer. They were very ineffective at best and quite often screwed up your ability climbing or trying to drag and use a hose line because there's just a little square metal box on your chest connected with a tube to a little face piece you had. We had that for quite a few years.

The self-contained breathing apparatus that we have today was in its infancy as far as major fire department use, but a legal case where one man was testing an SCBA and one man still had the old Burrell and they were side by side trapped in a fire. The guy with the old Burrell mask died of suffocation and the guy with the SCBA survived. Immediately there after, nationwide, fire departments started going to the SCBA. That's been improved over the years.

You started out with heavy, heavy steel cylinders as your air supply. Now you have a very lightweight aluminum that's fiberglass wrapped as your air supply cylinder. You can get them for sixty-minute supplies where the original ones were only thirty minutes. They were only a thirty minute rated unit. A heavy breathing guy got maybe twenty minutes out of it. A thin guy who didn't get heavily exerted doing a lot of work, might have gotten twenty-five minutes out of it. That was it.

Cody: We had the Burrells filter type masks when I came on in '64. We used them. Our captain insisted that we use them and he used his all the time so we always used them. As for the rest of the department, I don't really recall. But we did use them all the time. In '72 they took the Burrells off the rigs and gave us nothing. The truck companies had two SCBAs and a Chemox. No one wanted to use the Chemox because everyone was afraid of it. But the engines had no masks for a while until they bought MSAs, then they got Survive-airs and then we went to Scotts.

Garrity: They were using Burrells. You always used masks. Eddy Vesey and people like that in Five Truck were still working without the mask, but we always used it. We used them all the time. Small fires obviously you didn't. You'd go as far as you could without it and then you'd put it on. It made working a lot easier because there wasn't all that weight that you had with the new masks. You could get in. On a regular three story frame there was no problem. It's just when you got into the basements and there were low oxygen levels that the masks didn't work. Of course, we thought they were working. We were breathing all right, but the plastics weren't being filtered out by that mask. That's the only bad part about it.

The masks started to change after a lawsuit. I don't remember the exact date, but it was before 1978. It was a lawsuit where the wife of a firefighter who died using that mask sued a city. From what I understand they were declared unsafe for firefighting. The next day they came in and took all the filter masks away and we worked with two SCBAs and a Chemox mask. Those were the three masks we had on the truck. Those were the only masks in the house for a while. The engine might have had a Chemox. I used the Chemox mask in a cellar fire over here on Raymond Boulevard. I was scared to death of the damn thing because I could never get the lungs to fill up and work. But it worked. It worked for the half hour or forty-five minutes that I was using it. I also used it at a supermarket. I used it there too and it worked. So it worked, but I didn't have a lot of faith in it.

Then when we got the other masks everybody complained how heavy they were and how awkward they were, how hard they were to use, and how short a time they gave you. It says a half hour mask. On a good day you get fifteen minutes out of it and you have to change it. But it had to be a change for the better because all that shit going into that filter mask. We didn't know what it was, didn't care. The guys who wore the filter masks back then will still tell you it was a better mask. And in some ways I agree with them because you had it on when you went out the door. You put your coat on. You put your mask on and you went out the door with the rig. So when

92

you got there you didn't have to take the mask out of the compartment and put it on. You just went upstairs and went to work. If they could develop a mask that could filter out all that stuff it'd be perfect.

Knight: The Burrells were a good mask. They were a good all-purpose mask. You could wear them around your neck responding to an alarm. You get there. You grabbed your tool. You went into the building. Boom-boom, put the thing on and off you went. When they changed over to the SCBAs, the first ones we got were the MSAs and they were heavy. In a truck company or even an engine company, the gear you're wearing weighs roughly thirty-five, forty pounds and then to throw this thing on your back. You're trying to climb in windows with it. In a truck company a lot of times you were getting hung up on windows, on the window frames. I got hung up a couple of times on window frames with the tanks.

They were better. I'll grant you they were a better mask. They gave you more time in the fire and better air because you weren't breathing filtered air like you were with the Burrells. You were breathing clean fresh air, but it was just that they were so damn awkward. As the years went by they downsized them. They took the weight away from them. The ones we have now are lighter. They wear better. We have new face pieces, which give you better visibility. The other ones, the old ones we had, always seemed to fog up on you. You were forever trying to pull the mask away, trying to get the lens cleaned up. But over all, these are good masks now. When they first came out, like anything else, they were awkward. You have to go with the flow. You have to go with the changing times.

McGovern: We had the Burrell, each company had two SCBAs, but they were in the boxes and nobody ever used them. It was always the Burrell. I remember the Burrell, feeling how hot it used to get. You never really knew when it was saturated, but everybody wore them because they were light and easy to use. Then you'd come back. You'd change your canister and go back in service. Even then, I think a few guys in Twelve Engine at the time were wearing SCBAs exclusively, but back then they weren't the aluminum tanks. They were the heavy steel tanks and they were big. They were big and heavy. So guys would avoid them like the plague. As long as they could get away with a Burrell they would use that. I remember a lot of those Burrells getting saturated. You could feel the heat. You're drawing on them. To get a breath, you really have to pull it out of it. But that's my experience with the Burrells. They were easy, nice and light and easy, so everybody liked them.

The Squad also had Chemox masks. So, for certain jobs we would use them. They were a problem too. They got real hot. You had to dispose of them carefully. Put them in a bucket of water and puncture them. With the Squad we'd get the tip at some fires. "The Squad's here. Give them the tip and they'll take it in." that kind of thing. We've done that a few times. Chief Greeley was always doing that. As soon as we showed up, he'd scream in the doorway, "The Squad's here. Give them the tip." And we'd wind up taking it into the apartment. That was a common thing down there with Chief Greeley. It was mostly Down Neck that they did this. But they did it up above when guys were taking a beating. We'd be there with the masks on.

Prachar: You didn't have your SCBAs. You had your old Burrell. The only way you knew that was bad was by looking in the little glass window. If that changed colors, that meant the canister was bad, get rid of it. That's why when I came on, I very seldom wore that. Being in a truck company, going to the roof and everything, it hung in front of you. It was constantly in the way. I learned a lot from the captains who I worked with about how to skip breathe back then. Skip breathing is a method where you can breathe as you're working, holding your breath, and building up your lungs is what it came down to. You build up your lung capacity so they could hold enough air and you can breathe out as you're working very slowly, where you don't have to huff and puff just to keep breathing. You could hold your breath a little bit longer in the smoke, could take a chop in the roof to open the scuttle and get out.

With the skip breathing, it helps if your truck men get caught on the roof. There's only so much air you could get up there if you have a good smoky fire, sucking onto the roof, which we used to call it back then. Getting air, then you could get up and look and you could hold your breath longer. It's filling your lungs up to full capacity. Going back to about 1980 or so, we brought somebody into the department to show us how to skip breath. The old-timers knew that. They didn't have to be taught. That's what helped me a lot when I was working on the roof; the skip breathing, where to look for fresh air and all.

The idea was to make you work a little bit longer. You had your mask. In the early '70s they did away with the Burrell and brought in the SCBAs because you had one hundred percent fresh air. With the Burrells it was filtered air. And when the filter got dirty, that's when you looked into the little glass for the color change. All you were doing was breathing in filtered air. If someone had a bad canister, the mask would come off.

You would see guys just collapsing from smoke inhalation because they didn't wear their mask. The mask was there. You wore it going in, but it came off for one reason or another. But the guy would go right back to work. Come out, get some oxygen, go back to work, and later on end up with the headache and the nausea and everything. Back then you thought it was part of the job.

You would go back to the firehouse and the captain would tell you, "Lay down for an hour or so. Take a break." The captains took care of the men, to the point that if you did work hard at a fire and did collapse or whatever, the captain would tell you, "Go lay down. Do this. We're not going back in service for another hour." A lot of that was the chiefs. If the chief knew you were working hard, he would say, "Give your guys an extra hour."

Now fires are so far and few in between, that if a company's out on the road at one little thing and they hear a fire come in and they knew they would have gotten it, they'll jump the call. They'll say they'll take it, sending the covering company back. Back in those days, there weren't too many companies that could do that, because if you had a good fire you had to pick up the hose. You didn't put it back in the bed. You rolled it. Then you had to go back to the firehouse and hang it if you were working days. But they would give the guys a break if they knew you were busting hump for a while.

If you went to a fire Down Neck, down the port area, they had the SCBAs at the time because they might have had to go into the ships, down in the ship. So they had SCBAs on the rig. That eventually started working its way uptown. That's when the masks became heavy. There were companies that had them, maybe one a company or two a company. Everybody else wore the Burrells. But you did take a beating. Even with the mask on the next day you would wake up at home and say, "Boy do I have a headache." Your little glass window didn't say change the canister, so you didn't change it. Here today, they would just change the whole tanks. But yes quite a few guys went down. Now everybody has to wear their SCBAs up on the roof.

Your injuries, you probably had your injuries back then too, the same way. A guy would cut his hand or something and he would continue to work because he wanted to be with the rest of the guys. Maybe when he went back to the firehouse, he would show it to the captain. Then they would take you over to, at the time Martland hospital, have you stitched up and the guy would come right back to work.

In engine companies, the guy who had the tip, when he had air coming in, he didn't need his mask. They became known as the macho men. You were a macho fireman because you didn't wear a mask. Even today, I still find myself not putting the mask on. I'll have the tank and everything there, but I'll still hold my breath, go in, work then put my mask on at the last minute.

A lot of guys, guys who were in your busy companies up on the hill. They would get in there. Sometimes couldn't wait, just get in there, we'll get the mask. It used to be an unofficial procedure. You get there; the first guy stretches the line. Just to get the line in there. The other guys would start masking up. Now this guy is in there, he'll be taking a beating. Here's where your skip breathing comes in. He'll get that line as close to the fire as he can. Then when the guy comes in with the tank, he'll tap him on the shoulder and he'll go out and get his tank.

Once OSHA came in and said everybody has to have the SCBAs, then it was mandatory that every company get it. On Rescue, when we went down into the Port area, we had a full compliment of MSAs in case we had to go in to a chemical company or something along with our chemical suits. A couple of companies, Twenty-seven, Thirty-two, they had them because they were the first one's down into the Port area. So they had them, the SCBAs at the time, more or less to get in to see what they had. I don't remember how long it took, the complete change over, exactly who had them at what time.

Cosby: The masks, we had the old filter type masks. They were good to a certain extent. The thing I liked about them, they were light. You could perform your job faster, but later on I found out that they were hazardous to your health. They really didn't give you the full protection that the air tank type masks gave. But we managed to do the job with it.

McDonnell: We didn't wear masks, pretty much. It was very rare that you wore the mask. You really didn't get deep into a fire. You couldn't get to where you got with the mask. Guys would get down on the floor with the line, get in as far as they could, and hope somebody got in there and ventilated. You had a lot of ventilation. They would move in that way. We had a lot of fires in vacant buildings and they were opened. So, a lot of times the buildings were already vented. It wasn't like, in the occupied buildings where you had a lot of smoke before you could get to the fire. They thought they were getting in, that they were really going in there.

98

The mask was the Burrell. When we wore a mask, we used to wear the Burrell mask. We had the Chemox and the SCBAs on the truck. Chemox I used a few times over the years, with the canister. You'd pop the canister, breathe in, and inflate the bellows. It was a World War II mask. They used them in the Navy, probably for fighting ship fires, going down into the different holds. Supposedly you wore the SCBAs for cellar fires. I wore them a couple of times when I was in One Truck. The problem with them, they were so heavy. They had a glass front piece, which was the best front piece I ever wore. They were great. You could see. They didn't fog up on you.

But basically, we wore the Burrell. It had a little round blue disk with a stripe that was a different shade of blue. You were supposed to check it every day. When the stripe became the same color as the outer part, then the canister was no good. You had to get a new one. They were supposed to last up to a couple of hours. They were on the truck and you were supposed to check it, the same as you do today. Most guys didn't check it, just like they don't do today.

There was somebody, in either New York or California, a guy died, there was a lawsuit, and his family won the suit. That was the end of the Burrells. We went to the SCBAs. They were just heavy as all hell. They weighed forty or forty three pounds or something.

When we first got those masks a lot of guys got burned. I remember I got burned one time. I was sitting in the firehouse. Someone came in and we were talking. The guy said, "Gee, a whole lot of people are getting burned. What the heck? We never had guys getting burned like this." What it was, with that mask we were just going further into the fire than guys had been able to go before. You were getting caught. You were in a situation

99

that really nobody had been in before. The fire could go from here to there. When you were out where there was some air, you didn't get hit with that. Now, you were walking right into this heavy smoke and heavy heat. It took a lot of guys getting burnt to start to realize, "Gee." There was an adjustment period. If you go back and check the records, you'll find that after we started using the SCBAs, there were a lot of ears burnt, more than normal.

There are times you get in there and all of the sudden it gets pitch black. You have black smoke and you feel that heat. Then you know the fire's coming. It's close by. I think in the beginning guys didn't realize that. You were walking into a place that nobody had ever been before. So, we had a lot of burns. Until it happened to you and next time you were a little more aware of it. You knew something.

I think a lot more of using the line like in the old days and pour water on smoke. Back then we used to always be screaming, "Put the line on it." "I don't see the fire." "Put it on the ceiling." Because you didn't know where it was, but you knew it was coming. If you knew which direction it was coming from it would be okay, but a lot of times you didn't. You know the fire is somewhere, but you don't know where it is. You could tell it was coming. You only needed to get burned once like that, after that when that feeling came, you could recognize it. I knew I could recognize that until the time I left the job. That happened to me with Al Fraser when we got trapped. That's what happened. There was a definite adjustment to those masks. Then there was the weight. The heart attack rate had to skyrocket after using those masks.

Melodick: Compared to what we have now, the Burrell was wonderful. Light, easy to get off if you had to. It was never in your way. You didn't feel like you had twenty pounds on your back. Because it was only a few pounds and you had a face piece. That was it. For that reason it was great, but in the long run I guess obviously it wasn't because we'd still have them if it was. We had those for a few years and they did away with them. Then we got a different set up, which we have now.

I was in the firehouse when they took the Burrells off the rig. God, that goes back many years. I was like, "Why are they doing this?" I didn't know. I was fairly new. Because I thought it was the greatest thing. I said, "This is nice." Then when we got the new ones, I said, "These things are heavy." They felt like three hundred pounds compared to what we had. They were a pain in the neck putting on, taking off, and at a fire, getting through a window, a doorway, or whatever. The Burrells you just went right in, no problem. But you know like everything else, I guess we adjusted and it's better for you anyway than what we were using.

Pianka: We did use the masks. In the busier companies you did because you had to. I mean a lot of guys still didn't wear their masks. Some of the old timers still would go as far as they could without a mask and then they'd finally flip on the Burrell. In a busy company you had to end up using your mask. You were going to go in. That was just it. You were going to go into a spot where you couldn't breathe anyway, so it wasn't that great a change in that respect. You were putting something on which actually worked better for you in the long run. Then some fireman died in California if I recall correctly and his wife sued. They blamed the masks and that's when they went to the self-contained. We'd probably still be using the old Burrells if it wasn't for that.

They just came in one day and took them off the rig. It was at least a couple of weeks to a month until you had a full compliment of SCBAs.

There were a lot of guys fighting. They didn't want to do it. But I think we definitely operated better in the days of Six Engine when we were all using the masks and we're going in, it turned out to work pretty well. We did a bang up job.

Rotonda: The mask that we had was what they called the Burrell, the miners' mask that they pulled off the market all together. Then we went to the Navy masks, the Chemox that you were supposed to pump up and get going. It was a hassle to get those damn things going. Then we all started getting the SCBAs and everything else, but this was over a period of time.

The miners' mask, all it did was supposedly filtered out the carbon monoxide. But there are other gases. I assume that you still got some of it because it's a whole mixture of gases. Now with all the manmade materials they use, I guess the SCBA is the best thing to do, but still the bulkiness, the weight even though they cut down the weight of them. What's the weight now about twenty-five pounds? Somewhere in that area, it used to be more with the old bottles on them. Even with that cut down, you're still carrying a lot of weight on your body.

For a truckman it's very difficult to work, pulling ceilings and walls, with your tank on and everything else. So, as soon as you feel like there's enough air into the building, you pull off your mask when you can, because you can't work. Even though there's a lot of smoke and stuff burning. You have these plastics and everything still smoldering. You have to look up at the ceiling and pull the ceiling. You're banging your head. So the first thing you do, as soon as you have enough oxygen, you pull off your tank, you put it on the side, and you go to work. That's hazardous to the firemen themselves more then they realize. But you don't even think of these things when you're doing them. It's true. You're into a fire and you work at it.

The guys give like a hundred and ten percent at least. They're all breaking their ass. Then you're short men, so you're working your ass off. You're into a point where you're really beat to hell. You pull off the mask and you suck in all the garbage. This is what happens.

T. Grehl: There were old Chemox and Burrells. The Chemox was a little bit of a pain in the neck. You had to almost jump start it by breathing into it, holding the tubes. It was like a lung machine. I could never really get that right. The Burrell was a canister. I do remember that. It was a filter canister. And then, like two or three months after I came on they went to the SCBAs. They were basically the same concept as we have now, other than you didn't have your own face piece. We all shared a face piece. A little different design but basically that was the beginning of it.

Nobody really wanted to put that heavy, heavy tank on their back when they were used to the Burrells or the Chemox. They were very light. Just throw them on. The SCBA was such a pain to use that a lot of people got in the habit of not putting masks on. When they did put them on, they had a tendency of not using it until you couldn't basically breathe, until you really started coughing and choking. Then they would don the face piece and they would take it off fairly early. It was a big transition period.

It was a heavy, a lot heavier than what we have now. For some reason forty pounds with everything hits a bell with me, with the tank and the harness and everything. But it was a pain in the neck. Especially if you were going to put it on for thirty-five, forty minutes, crawl around and stand when you weren't used to it. The Burrells would be a fifteen-minute filter thing and you'd be fine. And the Chemox was an inflatable thing. The Burrells were almost like the old fashioned war things, like you see in the war movies. They almost looked like that.

We had both the Chemox and the Burrell on the truck because one, the Chemox was supposed to be for a longer period of time if you went down in a hole. But I think that was only for a year, not even a year. Then I think we went right over to what, basically, what we have now. But they were demand at the time. Now they're the positive flow. We were drilled on them. We were trained on them at the Academy.

I remember in the beginning they were popping like crazy with the water freezing in the diaphragms. That was a major problem. So, supposedly you had to clean that out after every use, clean out the wetness.

Ryan: The masks, a lot of the old timers tended to stay away from them or used them sparingly. We soon figured out you weren't doing your job right useless you were wearing your mask. The masks still, the MSA masks, there was some difficulty with them. They had a collapsible rubber breathing hose. There was a helix inside, but it often became detached.

Langenbach: The only thing we had different when I came on the job, we didn't have SCBAs. We still had the Burrell. That was only for a little while. And then the truck got issued what in the Navy we called them OBA, oxygen breathing apparatus, the Chemox mask. The captain had a little fifteen minute Scott bottle and then we got the MSA. Then we went MSA, to SurviveAir, to Scott. The Burrells weighed two pounds. The MSAs with the steel tanks were forty, but it was great because you could go a lot further with them. You could do a lot more with the mask on.

It was an interesting thing to see the change for the old timers, the guys who were old timers when I came on the job and how they reacted. "Now we're going to have to wear this mask." Like some guys flatly refused to wear them. Some engine companies would operate under the premise that one guy would run in there with the line as far as he could without a mask while the other guys were putting their masks on. I never saw the sense to that, but that's what they did, some people did that. And some people refused. Bob Schimph, I don't think I ever saw him with a mask on. Eddie Vesey, I mean these are guys that are like legends. To me they're legends, Vesey and Pete and Joe Lefcheck and those guys, never wore masks. Very rarely, I mean if they wore masks you knew we had some bad shit going on. Something was wrong.

Luxton: It was the old MSA self-contained. In the Academy they told you how to take the regulator apart and get the moisture out of it. I think the Burrells, the canister masks, had all been taken off by that time. They were around. I was familiar with them because we had some of them in Nutley. I think we had two or three SCBA's and some of the canister masks. The big thing was don't go into a basement because you needed oxygen. They might have had some of the Chemox, with the two lungs. Those were down at the Academy. They showed you how to use them. I think Nutley had a couple of them. For the most part we had MSA self-contained masks then and they were probably a couple of years old by then because the straps were really pretty torn up.

Connell: If you picked up on the respiratory protection standard from the way my captain left his mask on the rig and I sat outside the whole fire holding the mask in my hand, it shows you the mentality of wearing masks in those days. And the mentality I was broken into. Basically a mask was a thing to slow you down or to keep you out. Once you got in the building, if you had a mask on you were harassed for having the mask on. Candy-ass.

The masks were the MSA forty pound beasts. People could push amazingly far into a building without them. There was always somebody out there somewhere, who would rather be coughing and hacking. I'm getting ready to start barfing my lunch on the floor and they'd be there, "Come on, what's wrong with you. Go on." Holy shit, I'd be panting. Take a couple of real quick breaths, before actually committing yourself to a mask. Then go back in and anytime nobody is looking, take a couple of more to keep up with everybody.

But unfortunately through my whole career on the fire department that mentality stuck with me. Later on in time I became basically one of the last ones to put a mask on, one of the first ones to take it off. And I took pride in how much black shit I could cough up on my three days off.

Langevin: When I was first assigned we had old type SCBAs with full-face pieces not the two eyeholes, extremely heavy. I think, rough estimate, the whole thing weighed thirty-five, forty pounds. A lot of the old timers wouldn't wear a mask. The masks were there for your use. I guess it was entirely up to you if you wanted to use them or not. Nowadays, it's almost mandatory, but back then if you didn't need one or want one you didn't have to put it on.

Pignato: We had MSA's which were heavy. They weren't positive pressure just regular masks. I was already a certified diver, so I was use to wearing compressed air. It wasn't a big deal for me. I've been scuba diving since I was in high school. It was heavy. As soon as you could get the damn thing off, you took it off. The trouble is at a fire, if it was still going, you wind up with smoke inhalation. The first time I was brought to Martland Hospital with smoke inhalation, I was semi-conscious. I don't remember going to the hospital. I remember being dragged into the emergency room. It was my first year.

I'm in the hospital. I'm lying in a big ward. There's this guy alongside me. I look at him. I have oxygen on. I'm starting to get my faculties back. I'm looking at this guy, he's not breathing. I say, "uh-oh." It's like in a dream where you call for help and nobody comes. I'm yelling trying to get the nurse's attention. She finally comes over and says, "You firemen are always getting hurt and always a lot of trouble. What's the trouble?" "This guy ain't breathing." She says, "Where did he come from?" I say, "EMS brought him in." "Well, nobody told me." "Yeah, so." I'm out of it anyway.

She gets a code blue and they all come running with the crash truck and all that stuff. They pull the curtain. I opened the curtain up, I was watching anyway. They had metal braces. Every time they zapped him, you heard ca-ching, ca-ching . The doctor was worried because he's responsible for that guy dieing. The guy died and they packed him off. Chief Marasca finally came around and he says, "What did the doctor say?" Because I was a new red-ass, he wanted to make sure I was okay. I says, "What doctor?" He started raising hell in that hospital. He raised Cain. Finally there were doctors all over the place, jabbing me, twisting to do a blood gas test. They took my blood gas and all that stuff.

Perdon: We had the MSAs. They weren't positive pressure. There's a world of difference. Even with that you took a beating. You just got so much shit from the side, but it's just like anything else. You didn't know any better. It was easy. They were heavy sons of a bitches compared to the composites that we got after that. I forget the exact weight. They were all you knew up until that point, that's what you work with. And the weight, you never questioned it. That's just, that's part of the job. You had to put that tank on whatever it was made of. Not until better things came along did you know how much you were working with.

Ricca: It was just after the change over from the Burrell to the MSAs. But it was the black face piece like the frogman's face piece. I never thought I'd be able to wear it because when I was visiting the firehouse, Joe put a Burrell on me and I panicked. I was, I guess about seventeen, eighteen at the time. All I did, I just ripped it off my face. It stuck with me and I was afraid when I got into the Academy that I wouldn't be able to wear a mask. Captain McDonnell was very big with the masks. Captain Calvitti was good with the masks. I had Captain Titcomb. They kind of pushed the fact that you must wear it. You had to have it on. Later on in my career is when I kind of shied away from it.

But it was a simple mask to put on. The warning bell was on your belt. I think it was on your right side. I liked to check it. You unscrewed the regulator and there were two arms and a diaphragm. If you cleaned your diaphragm, you had to put the arms back in the right direction or the mask would lock up on you. It wouldn't work. That's what I remember of the masks.

The only time I used a Burrell was when Joe put it on me. But the thing is that there were still Burrells left on the truck. I guess guys snuck them because guys were still wearing them. I thought, never really using it in a fire, I thought it was a great mask for the roof men to use. Just to have it in case because I never wore a tank going to the roof. I never felt comfortable working with it. The Burrell was something you have over your shoulder. Bang, if you needed it, it was there. You wouldn't think twice about carrying it. Actually, I wonder if someday they could ever have something not like the Burrell, but something you could have when you're talking about high rises, you could carry it with you. Even an escape type mask, something like that possibly. The cub was another mask. Everybody used to wear one when you acted. It was a small tank. You just take it and throw it over your shoulder like it was nothing. You didn't even know it was on you. But then they outlawed that I think because of the time.

Gesualdo: They were MSAs when we first came here with demand regulators, flexible, low pressure hose, which ran from the regulator to the face piece. I remember that being a problem with the collapse, though they did come out later on with the wire in the low pressure hose. I think when I first came on they weren't wired. They didn't have the reinforced wire in there, so they collapsed very easily. Shared face pieces. Everybody used pretty much the same face piece or whoever used that breathing apparatus. Cumbersome, but not where it's to the point where you didn't want to use it because of the weight. Restrictive only, I can remember being restricted a lot of times going through windows. They didn't have the hinged harness like they have today. Canvas straps and no Personal Alarm System alarm. That's pretty much it.

That was at the time when a lot of older guys on the job, rough and tough types, refused to use it. They put it on, but I remember, very rarely seeing a Battalion Chief with a breathing apparatus on. Some captains, I'd say probably fifty/fifty at that point. I think our class in '78, it was reinforced; the fact that it is the best piece of equipment they've ever developed in the fire service. But I remember probably about fifty/fifty. I used mine religiously during the knock down. I guess everybody was guilty of taking it off during overhaul, which is a mistake, but that's pretty much how it went.

Chapter Five: Hose and Nozzles

Fredette: We only had a booster hose and two and a half line. That was all. We didn't have a shut off nozzle. It was just an open nozzle. When you got your water, you got your water. Seventeen Engine was the first one that got the inch and a half. That was in the 1950's. Rusheck never liked that because he was an old timer. They were used to that booster with that two and a half back up. The newer Deputy Chiefs, the younger men, they used to swear by that inch and a half. But Rusheck was more of a two and a half man. He would say, "You know Frenchy, guys are depending too much on that inch and a half. They are going to get caught some day." But they put out a lot of fire with that inch and a half.

Vetrini: We had no inch and a half. All our fires were fought with two and a half inch hose. Very seldom would you go into a building with a booster. Maybe if it was a mattress, but even then they didn't take a chance. You backed up a booster with a two and a half line immediately. You had better have a two and a half inch line laid.

Redden: We carried ten and ten, twenty lengths. It was a divided hose bed and it was all two and a half inch hose. No inch and a half at that time. We had a booster and hard suction. We used to use the hard suction once a month for training purposes, but never used it at a fire.

The hose-well at Two Engine was pretty high because it was a three-story building. Most of the firehouses are two stories. The junior firefighters had to take care of that. The old-timers, they weren't about to climb that ladder. But I had no problem with it. I had no problem what so ever.

The hose-well had a ladder going up the wall, straight up the wall. Up at the top you had a platform and then you had a place that you would hang the male coupling in. You'd slide it in there. They would bring the hose up to you on a pulley, on a rope. They'd hook it up about five feet from the end. So they'd bring it up and you'd grab it, put it in the connection, and then unloosen the rope and send it back down. Sometimes you would lose a length while you were sliding it on and it would fall straight down. It's happened, but thank God it never happened with me.

They had a position called the drillmaster when I came on. He was essentially in charge of equipment and training. He brought this Navy nozzle, the Rockwell, down to us. It was made of aluminum. You could have a straight stream, a fog steam, and could also have used it with an applicator. He gave it to me and said, "This is the Navy nozzle. You can do this, you can do that, but don't use it because it's very fragile. It'll break." That's what he told me. Of course we used it when we had to.

Kinnear: Back then all the hose had to be hung. The hose-well had to be sixty feet tall because the hose lengths are 50 feet. It had a door at the top and a ladder going up the side. One man had to climb that ladder. It was usually the youngest guy until the youngest guy finally said, "Hey, wait a minute. Somebody else take a turn." So I went up there quite a few times. There was a metal platform up on top and there were brackets that the hose slid into. There was a rope. The guys down at the bottom would attach the hose to the rope and they would pull it up. When it got to the top, you put it on one of the brackets, detached the rope, and let the rope back down again.

After every fire, every time you wet the hose, you had to hang whatever you stretched. If you stretched six lengths, you had to go up, drop six lengths down to put on the apparatus, and put the six that were wet up. You would leave them up there for two, three days, or four days. After they were dry you'd drop them, roll them, and store them in the back. It was quite an experience going up there. I don't know if I'd do it today. Probably would, but I'd be scared because it was high. Every month, supposedly, if you didn't use the hose, you were supposed to put a new load on. Take the ten or twenty that were on the rig off. We could get away with just changing where the creases were, but a lot of captains insisted that you take the ten and hang them. Get the folds out of them; put a new ten or twenty on. Six didn't do that much because we got the work. The hose got changed by itself because you stretched.

They didn't have inch and a half. It was strictly two and a half inch hose. We probably got inch and a half in the late 50's. But you had a choice when I went on of a one-inch booster or a two and a half inch line. It was tough, but you had better roll calls then. Most of your companies had at least one and four, some of them had one and five, some even one and six. So pulling two and a half was a lot easier.

You had ten lengths in each side of the bed. One would be male coupling out and one would be female out. You chose whichever one you wanted. If you were stretching from a hydrant, you took the female and hooked it up to the hydrant. You tried to stretch with the rig if you could. But if you were stretching fire to hydrant, you'd stretch the male end with a nozzle from the rig. We had no pre-connected hose. There was no such thing. We only had a hundred gallon booster tank on that first rig.

It certainly changed. Inch and a half made for a quicker attack on the fire naturally. We were wearing masks even though it was the all service mask. I think you got into the heart of the fire a lot quicker with the inch and a half. The only problem with it was that some companies thought they could use inch and a half all the time, in every type of fire. When you had a

112

big three-story frame going and you weren't really doing well with an interior attack, some companies would still go for inch and a half for outside firefighting. That didn't work. You needed the big volume of water.

F. Grehl: After you used the hose, you would pick it up, put it on the back step, and go back to the firehouse. All the wet, dirty hose was taken off and put in the hose-well. We had an unwritten rule in most of the busy companies. If you used it at night, you took the surplus supply and put it back on the rig. The daytime crew would then take the hose out, clean it, and hang it in the well. Whoever worked three days later in the daytime would take it down, sweep it off, roll it up, and put it back in the supply. It's supposed to dry for seventy-two hours. Nobody liked to do that.

We had what they called a half hose-well in the back of Six Engine. We used to tie a rope around the hose about midway, take it up and hang it over the loop up there. So, it would hang twenty-five feet on each size. The thing was thirty feet, thirty-five feet high at the most. Most of the hose-wells were sixty feet high. You had to go up that inside ladder fifty feet and hang the hose by the coupling. There were very few of the half wells. People would take turns going up. "Who was last in the hose-well?" Now it's your turn in the well today. If you were in the well, you didn't have to make the rig. They didn't want you rushing down that ladder. That was a lousy job.

McCormack: When I came on the job the only kind of hose we had was a two and a half and a booster. In those days we didn't have fog nozzles and we didn't have inch and a quarter lines. We had the two and a half inch lines, boosters, and master streams. We didn't have fog, we had straight play pipes.

We had hard suction on the apparatus. We didn't do much drafting, although we drilled in drafting constantly. Everybody had to drill in drafting. You had to be certified at least once a year. The pumpers were tested once a year to make sure they could draft water. If they couldn't draft, they were fixed so they could draft water. It was part of the Underwriters' requirements. The idea was, if we had a conflagration and we had to look for a water supply because the main hydrant system was disrupted we would use the hard suction. It was thought we could always get our water from the Passaic River, Branch Brook Park Lake, or Weequahic Park Lake.

Masterson: If you had a fire, you'd take the hose back and throw it in the hose-well. In the morning, going to work, you'd peek in the hose-well. See what they did last night. See if they left you a big pile. Then you'd haul it all up, dry it so many days. They put the date when it went up on a board. Then you'd come in. You knew which day it had to come down. We'd be sitting at the table. Somebody would say, "The hose's got to come down." Okay. So, you'd bring the hose down. You'd stretch it out on the apparatus floor. You'd sweep it with a stiff broom, cleaned it all up and then it was rolled up and put in the back on the stockpile.

Every length of hose on the apparatus had a number. Every time when you were loading after you came back from a fire, loading dry hose, you had to give the number there. They wrote the number on the board. So, all the numbers of the hose on the wagon and on the engine, all the numbers meant they were there. When they were checking on hose, you'd go down and check all the butts, get the numbers. Look on the board and get their numbers. Look at the stock; you knew where every length of hose was.

114

Then they changed it around where you throw it on wet. They put that Dacron or nylon or something. The hose was wet and dirty, full of glass. That was another bad thing; you'd get cut from the glass on the hose. That's why we put it down on the floor and brushed it with a stiff broom.

It was two and a half, when I first went on that's all we had was two and a half and a booster. Then we got the inch and a half which was a big boost on the wagon. Everything was with that two and a half, but that was a lot of work, especially when it got wet. Before that got water you had better get all that you needed and get it to where you wanted it because once that gets charged with the water, one or two guys have an awful job moving it around. Especially going up the stairway in a two story frame with a two and half inch charged, you're not going up too far. An inch and a half you can handle it. Booster you can handle it. We had those one inch boosters, they were great. Then of course later on the John Beam came in with that pressure stream. I got burnt more times with that sucker, steam burns.

Deutch: They had a lot of big hose Down Neck for all the rubber fires. There were large fires in the rubber yards and the brush three or four times. They stretched the big lines. In fact, I think Sixteen Engine had the record in those years for stretching line. They were always washing hose and drying them. They always had their hose-well full of hose.

Freeman: When I came on the job we had inch and a half. I remember we used to use the two and a half with the wye. So, inch and a half was in '56. If you were first due you'd hook right up to your inch and a half and you'd go right in. The firefighting was not much different than it is today. You had the filter type mask and you used basically the same methods. They have refined all the different operations today, but then they were basically the same. You'd go in, put the fire out. If it got too hot, you backed off. You overhauled the same way.

The hose-well was unique. I still have the iron piece that they hung the butts on. It must have come down from the well. I think I still have it in my locker. I don't know if they have that in the museum. I think I'm going to give that to the museum, a piece of equipment from the past. The hose-well, that's how we dried the hose many moons ago. We'd come from a fire and we always had extra hose that was numbered to keep track of each length. We used two and a half for the feed and we had inch and a half. All the hose had numbers on the butts. We had a board in the back behind the apparatus with all the numbers.

We also had a table made from round piece of wood that came off a wire reel or something like that and was attached to a concrete traffic stand. The table would turn. We would put the hose on there so you didn't have to drop it. After a while they lost it or it broke. Then we just threw the hose on the ground, flaked it out, and put it on the rig.

After a fire, we would take all the wet hose off. It was double cotton-jacketed hose then. You couldn't leave that on the apparatus because it would get moldy and then it would get rotten. Rotten hose would burst under pressure. So we had to hang it in the hose-well. The hose-well was at least fifty-five feet. You had to go in and climb all the way to a platform. You had a half-inch rope with a hook on the end that went over a wheel. The rope had to be seventy-five or a hundred feet long. We would take the dry hose down. That hose was heavy, cotton jacketed hose. You put the rope around the hose and attached the hook to the rope by the butt. Then you had to pull it down to take the hose out of the slot. You lifted it up and then the guys downstairs they would take it out on the apparatus floor. You would hold the rope. They would slowly take the hose out and lay it all out on the floor.

Then we would pull the wet hose up. Hook the rope around it and the guy downstairs would haul it all the way up to the top. You'd have to hook the butt into the receptacle there. Sometimes you'd get up there, hook the hose onto the rope and for some reason it would slip, and down would come the hose. All the way down. "Look out!" You'd have a length that went "Ththth" all the way to the bottom. Now you had to go down to the basement and open the door and bring the hose up. That's how you had to do it every time you had a job. You couldn't leave it on the apparatus.

Now if you had a lot of fires, then there wasn't any dry hose or the hose hadn't dried yet. You'd have to take down whatever was in the well. In the wintertime, if you took up the hose and it was frozen, you'd just piled it on top of the apparatus. You couldn't really bend it because it would crack the hose because it was frozen. That's really history. Maybe they can put a hose-well in the fire museum.

McGee: We didn't have inch and a half hose. We only had two and a half inch hose, so when you went to a bedroom fire on the second floor that's what you stretched up those steps. It was much more difficult which again accounts for why there were many more men in the company. Very seldom do I remember riding less than one and four in those companies. That might have been a problem in other companies, but in the busier companies I'm sure they tried to keep them fully staffed because we did have to stretch two and a half inch hose. The supply line hose was also two and a half inch. There was no three-inch supply line or four-inch supply line. The booster hose was like three quarter inch hose.

So everything got better which resulted in losing some manpower. The equipment was now doing the work of some of the men. Nozzles had straight bore tips. There certainly weren't any John Bean type of stream nozzle or anything else like that. It was straight bore tips that were not switchable to fog and a two and a half inch line. We didn't have the inch and a half yet. If you worked off the booster tank you would only get about forty-five seconds of water. I don't remember doing that too often, but usually if you had the line in place and the guy had nothing else to do but give you the water while he was waiting for a water supply then use what you had.

Most of the time you would stretch a booster, but you would be surprised. If somebody saw you stretching a booster in, like the first due company, you would stretch a two and a half inch line to back it up. Maybe not charge it, but you would stretch it. It was usually the same safe guards that are in place today. In most companies if they see people with a booster, they'll stretch an inch and a half. They switched to inch and a half prior to the riots. So it had to be in that time frame between '57 and '67, somewhere in there, maybe in the early '60s. I'm just guessing. They went from the two and a half to the inch and a half.

McGrory: We had inch and half hose by then. Inch and a half hose we started to use more, but anything that looked big they still tried to stretch two and a half in, especially some of the older captains. My captain still had a tendency, if he thought it was anything, he'd start stretching a two and a half. Sometimes you'd beat yourself because the guys who knew would start inch and half. They'd go right around you and put a lot of fire out.

Freda: When I first came on the job, there was a lot of two and a half inch line used because the manpower was there. There were a lot of long stretches made. A fifteen length stretch was nothing for me. It was nothing to take a hydrant. The cardinal rule in those days was you better have your own water. If you had to stretch three blocks to have your own water, that's what it would take. There was no running a line into the pumper. The pumper was the first stretch. You were never to be seen at a fire without your pumper being hooked up to a hydrant. That was a cardinal rule, even if you went to a second alarm for fire. You would find a hydrant to hook up to.

Charpentier: There were a few select companies that had inch and a half hose, pre-connected, but not everybody had. I think Six had it, Eighteen had it, Twenty had it, Twelve had it, and maybe Nine Engine had it up in the Third Battalion. It was just starting to come into use around then. That's when some of the chiefs went for pre-connected line. Before you had to wait until you got there, then stretch your line and hook your hose to the pumper.

When they changed from the double-jacketed cotton hose, you could just drain the water out of it and reload it right back into the hose bed, which saved a lot of time getting back in service. You didn't have to do the double work of rolling the hose up, taking it back, unrolling it, hanging it up in the hose-well and then putting dry hose back on the rig. It eliminated you having almost a double quantity of each size hose.

I would say in the late '70s and early '80s you started seeing four-inch hose and inch and three quarter hose. In the late '80s, early '90s you started seeing five inch. Not only that, they went to the real soft lining hose. It almost cut half of the weight off each length of hose.

Dunn: When I came on the fire department, we were using all two and a half inch hose in the industrial area and very limited use of inch and a half hose. We had open tip nozzles, straight tip nozzles, which you couldn't control the flow pattern as much.

When I was transferred up above to the upper battalions, we used two and a half inch hose very seldom except for feed lines. We used all inch and a half type of hose. Our hose line, which was an inch and a half line with a hundred gallon nozzle, over the years, has been upgraded now to inch and three quarter hose and two hundred gallon nozzles. So, I've seen the whole hose evolution on the Newark Fire Department change over my career. We went from two and a half inch feed lines to four inch feed lines and two and a half inch hand lines to inch and a half and now inch and three quarter lines with two hundred gallon nozzles which was a big upgrade.

The reason we went to inch and three quarter hose was that we could put more water on a fire on the back porch with limited manpower. That has worked, but there are a limited number of our applications for this hose. One of the quandaries that I've seen in the equipment change in the hose evolution was as we increased the size of the hose and the gallons of water we were moving and were asked to move, we were reducing our manpower. I believe it's the Oklahoma book that tells you every time you increase the amount of water you're using you give up mobility and you give up the advantage of a light weight, quick attack line because it's harder to move.

Now that we have all of our apparatus equipped with inch and three quarter hose and one company with two inch hose as our quick attack lines to give us a heavy flow of water, they reduce our manpower. I thought if we still used inch and a half lines we would have better mobility. We would have been able to get just as good if not better a knock down than we did with the inch and three quarter hose only because of the manpower. If you give us the same crews of one and three and one and four, the inch and three quarter hose would have been an asset. But now that we're riding half our companies probably one and two which gives us one man moving this line. You try to move a line around and try to move two hundred gallons of water. You lose mobility.

While we've made some strides in changing our equipment, I don't know if we've really made effective strides. If we go to a large three story frame back porch fire, the inch and three quarter hose does an excellent job. If we go to the fourth floor of an apartment building with a one and two and the guy charges the line on the first floor, he doesn't get to the fire floor because he doesn't have the manpower to do it. So, there's a give and take. That's probably the biggest change I've seen in the fire department, the hose evolution. We've changed every part of our hose evolution on our pumper today.

Carragher: We had cotton hose and that used to be a problem sometimes. Nine Engine had a fifty foot hose-well or a sixty foot high tower. Everything hung by a coupling. Twenty Engine had to double up. They had a short hose tower. Everything was folded in half. But you did go up and hang the hose. If you came in three or four days later, you had to pull everything off the rig that was wet and put a dry load on. That's the way you did it. They used to try to shake the red ass up the well, but I liked climbing. I didn't mind that. I thought that was easier than pulling hose up. So, you'd go up the well and they'd pull the hose up. You'd hang it and dry it.

The hose was all recorded. You could tell from the blackboard where on that rig what length of hose was. Everything was kept by number and date. You'd put on the board where the hose was, the first length, the second length. You knew exactly on the rig where that length of hose was. This continued up until the riots. Well, prior to the riots I guess some of the companies were starting to slip a little bit. But up until the riots you did that. And then we got a dryer and then the synthetic hose. The synthetic hose probably came in around the mid to late '60s. When we got the synthetic and you didn't have to dry it. Although at first we did dry that, if it was wet we used to hang it. But then gradually they found out you didn't have to do it. So they could save hose by only giving you the one load. Then you gradually went to the synthetic. You didn't have to reload.

Prior to that, you had a minimum of two loads of hose. We used to carry twelve and twelve of the two and a half, twelve on the male side, twelve on the female side. Inch and a half, we probably had maybe a dozen lengths. And that's what you carried. You had the same thing again on the side, on the skid so that it was dry. So when you came back from a fire you could change hose.

The two and a half was the heavy hose and inch and a half was the attack line mostly and the booster. Now Twenty was one of the first ones in the city that had a one inch booster. Which if you have the one inch booster and you have the right pressure, it gave you a good stream. Some of the earlier boosters gave you ten gallons of water. Sometimes they were just trickles. I remember the first one-inch booster that Twenty Engine got. It gave you a nice stream. The older firemen used to talk about going in with a booster for a working fire. Knock down a couple of rooms with a booster because you only carried seventy-five gallons of water in the tank. They did that while they were hooking up the hose. You didn't want to run out of water. So the guy grabbed the booster real fast, got in, swirled it around a little bit, and darken down a couple of rooms.

We had pre-connected inch and a half at Twenty. We used to stretch it into the building with masks and the inch and a half line, knocking the fire down while working off the tank. The advantage with the hose wagons was they used to carry three hundred gallons. In fact, Twenty Engine's hose wagon when I left there had a five hundred gallon tank. It was the only one in the city with five hundred, but the older hose wagons had three hundred gallons and I think the Ward LaFrances a hundred and twenty gallons or a hundred and twenty-five gallons.

So with a two piece company, the advantage of attacking the fire with your hose wagon and stretching in with the hose wagon was quick water. It was just a matter of hooking up to the other rig and getting a hydrant. You had water right away. It was quick water with a two-piece company done right. And it worked out that way. So you did attack fires with inch and a half getting right in like that working off the tanks. It was nothing for a good driver to pull back four lengths of hose to go to a hydrant. So, you'd go right to the building, take the front door and the driver would drag four lengths, hook up to the hydrant himself, and give you water, one man evolution.

We got three inch when I was a captain at Six Engine. I'm trying to think when because I remember the first fire I had with three-inch hose. I'm not sure if it was '66 or '67 when we got three-inch hose. I had a good fire somewhere over either down off Avon Avenue, Johnson Avenue, Avon Place, or one of those little streets over there. It was a three alarm. We dragged in a three-inch hose. Figured we'd give this thing a good shot with big water. We put a nozzle on three-inch hose. We charged that and had all we could do to hold that sucker. We said, "Oh boy we've got to throttle this one down."

It was going to be a supply line, but we did a lot of experimenting in those days. Today everybody has their fixed routine. Then we did everything we could ourselves. Like, "What's the fastest way to get water here? How can we do this?" Everyone knew if you heard of something, if somebody's tried something, you'd find out, what did they do? How did you do it? We'd be working on couplings all the time. How can we make a change in certain things? That's it. We tried it. Got three-inch hose, let's try it. We went to work with it. Hey, maybe we can knock something down. We were always looking for a bigger hose.

When I first came on we had the Rockwood nozzle, the Navy type nozzle that was a straight stream and a fog. The fog was not that real, real good on it. It was a good nozzle because of that knock down with the straight tip. But then you started getting the PDQ's and the better nozzles and they worked well.

They had some nozzles that were similar to the PDQ's, but it seemed the improvements came in the mid-60s and early-70s. They started coming up with the better nozzles. You get more water out of them. I liked the Rockwood over the older nozzles because you could go into a room, put it on straight stream, break it up off the ceiling, and operate. Probably it was in the '70s, when we got the real good nozzles, the attack nozzles that we use today.

Cahill: We were still hanging hose. Newest guy on the block went up the tower and you did that until another new guy came in the company. You're the guy who went up. I don't remember when they stopped doing that. Some companies got the hose driers, not all of them. That never worked out too well. But that was the first improvement they made. Then they went to the synthetic hose. I was at Five Engine then.

Highsmith: In those days we had hose that we had to hang in the hose-well. They didn't dry out themselves like they do now. We had to roll up our hose at the scene, take them back to the firehouse, throw them in the hose-well, reload with new hose, and if it was during the day, we would have to climb up in the hose-well, which is about fifty feet up, and we would have to pull the hose up there and let them dry out for three or four days, marking on the blackboard when they were put up. The next tour would come in and take them down, roll them back up, and put them back in the rack. So, it was work, but it was a lot of fun. You made a game out of doing it with no problem, so things went along easy.

It was always what they called red asses, new guys like me, who climbed up the hose-well, but it was no problem. As a matter of fact, I'd rather be up because when you're down you have to do the pulling up. Up the hose-well all you have to do is grab it, hook it on the hook, and release the rope and it goes back down.

Butler: On the engine companies you had only two and a half and three inch hose for many years then all of the sudden the advent of inch and a half hose came along. And any of that hose used in any fire still had to be hung up in the hose-well to dry. Unlike today, where you have four inch hose and one line is a great feeder. All your hose today is manufactured so that it can be reloaded wet right back on to the apparatus and ready for the next fire.

You have inch and three quarter today which I believe is about the mainstay in the Newark Fire Department. The way it's constructed and the nozzles that they're using today, it gives you water that's equal to damn close to a two and a half inch line. It's a lot more maneuverable, a lot easier to stretch, a lot easier to pull when wet, when it's charged. So, there have been improvements.

Cody: At that time we had the cotton jacket, double coat jacket rubber lined hose, which had to be hung and dried after every use. So, what you would do is when you came back from a fire or when you took up at a fire, you rolled all your hose, piled it on the back step, stood on top of that, brought it back to the firehouse, and hung it. And reload with all dry hose. The wet hose hung for a couple days; then you had to take it down, roll it, and store it. So, it was something that was part of your house duties every day where this was done. It made taking up a lot longer than what we do now just loading the synthetic jacket hose up. We had an inch and a half hand-line, four lengths and three lengths, and the booster is three quarter inch.

Garrity: It was double jacket, rubber lined, heavy hose inch and a half, two and a half. We didn't have three inch yet. We were just coming into the adjustable nozzles. I don't remember for sure, but I know we were using the adjustable fog straight stream nozzles back when we started. They had done away with the straight bore.

Cosby: We had the old type hose. It was the type that you had to climb up in the hose-well to hang it to dry. Otherwise, it rotted fast. The hose today is maybe twice as good. They don't hang hose anymore to dry.

D. Prachar: The hose-well, back in those days as compared to now, now you have hose you just repack, go to the next fire. Back then you had the cotton. Everything had to be hung for three days after a fire. You only carried two and a half and inch and a half. Low man on the totem pole had to climb all the way up the tower to hang. They would get caught up there when an alarm came in. Being the young guy, the one time that I did get caught up there, I wanted to go. By the time I got down, being that your roll call was one and four, one and five at the time, they would leave the guy who was in the well behind. And if it was a fire, he would jump in his car and go because he wanted to be at the fire.

The hose-well was fun, at times hilarious. They had little slits you had to put the butts into. If you had the hose fall out on you, everybody down below would yell and scream obscenities. One time a buff came in the house who we didn't like, so we showed him the hose-well. We hooked him up to the hook that went up about ten foot and let him hang in there for a while. Guy learned to keep his mouth shut when he was in the firehouse. The hose-well was used for numerous things.

If a tour had a fire the night before, the day tour always hung the hose. Every hose number was placed on the board, on a blackboard; where it was on the rig; whether it was on the pumper or the wagon if you had a two-piece company; where it was sitting; whether it was the first length on the bottom or the fourth or fifth length. If they wanted to check that length, you would look at the board and know exactly how far down you would have to go to get to that length. When that length went up in the hose-well, it was marked under the side of the board, hose-well. When it was down and rolled, where it was located. You always kept a count in the firehouse. Now, I would probably say, sixty, seventy percent of your hose-wells are all used for barbecue pits, smokestacks.

Pianka: At the time it was inch and a half. It was already past the stage where they switched over to inch and half. I guess for a number of years by that point. And then after about five years, they switched over to the inch

127

and three quarter, which initially was tough because my captain believed in a lot of water on a fire. That's what's going to save you. That was the main thing he stressed, "Leave the line open. Don't ever shut the line down." You shut the line down, that's it. You have nothing else, other than to know where the door is. But with the line he could always protect you.

He used to like to have the engine pump at a fairly high pressure. We were used to doing at least one seventy-five to two hundred pounds with the inch and a half. Now when we went to inch and three quarter, we were still pumping at that one seventy-five. I'll tell you the back pressure was difficult. Finally we moaned enough where he compromised. We went to one fifty to one seventy-five, in that area, because it was just too much. That was a good move.

The best move since I've been on the job that they did was going to the SCBAs, the inch and three quarter, and the increase in the water in a lot of these tanks. We had the Squirt here at Seven, which only had three hundred. Now we have seven hundred fifty gallon tanks on the engines as opposed to five hundred. So, when you first got to a fire you had those extra two, three minutes. That was like a lifetime. You could work off that tank and not worry about getting a feed for a long time.

T. Grehl: The nozzles were a slight variation, but they weren't like what we have now. They were the PDQ and had a black piece of rubber around the front. I guess Six Engine and a couple of other companies had that John Bean, a couple of other various nozzles, but I never worked with any of that.

We were still hanging hose when I came on. We went to four inch in the City of Newark in 1980. The reason I remember that is I was in One Engine and One Engine along with two other companies had a trail period.

We had the first trial on the four-inch hose. That replaced the three inch after 1980, so I do remember that date. We did the trial.

The four inch yellow hose was given to One Engine because we always went on the second alarm and always had to bring in water. This was "Let's experiment." The stuff was great. It was unbelievable. It was a little heavy until you learned the little ways of getting the air out and re-loading it and everything, but the stuff was great.

Langenbach: Twelve Engine had a hose drier, but it never worked, so we had to hang everything in the hose-well. That was interesting. I'd talk to people when I was down at the Academy teaching. Tell somebody about the hose-well. "Yes, you came back from a job and you had to pull hose up in there and take hose down." What are you talking about? We had to do this because of what?

Yes, you'd come back, especially if you were in the busy houses like Twelve and Six. You'd come back and you're dragging anyway and now you have to take hose down. Somebody has to climb to the top of the hose-well and hang hose back up again. This was all the inch and a half cotton jacketed and the two and a half inch. I think we just had inch and a half and two inch and a half. I don't think there was three inch yet. That came later. Twelve had a table. It was a big metal plate and it had a spike in the middle. You set the length of hose on there and you just reeled it right off. The nozzles were PDQs. Then when the inch and three quarter came in we went to the SM-15 and then the thirty after that.

Luxton: We had inch and a half line with PDQ tips. It was a one piece nozzle. It wasn't a two-piece like we have now. We had the two and a half with the play pipe on it and a load of three inch. One was hydrant to fire.

The other was fire to hydrant. You stretched both beds and you still hung hose then. You were starting to get some of the nylon hose in there, but it was mixed up and they had brass couplings. You didn't have the Pyro-lite. The hose was heavy.

When you came back from a fire, if you had wet hose, you dumped it on the floor. Put new dry hose on, so you could get ready to go back in service. Then somebody went up into the top of the hose tower. When I was new I'd climb up the hose-well. They'd haul it up and you'd take it off and hang it. They had a pulley arrangement with a hook on it. You'd put the hook on the center of the hose and pull the center of the hose up. The tower was twenty-five feet high or thirty-five, something greater than half the hose line. The hose hung in the middle, so two twenty-five foot pieces hung down. It would drip dry and you had natural ventilation because the well was open at the top, so the warm air in the firehouse would go up and dry the hose in twelve or twenty four hours.

In the mornings you'd take that stuff down, roll it, and put it on there so you'd have a fresh load. You had a cart to put it on. There was also a carriage that held hose. It had a big round platter off to the side and it would twirl around. You could actually roll the hose there by feeding it and turning it around. Most of the time you had wet hose anyway because you're going from fire to fire to fire. After a while we had mostly the Dacron and nylon hose and you didn't have to hang it anymore. The cotton jacket stuff disappeared.

Connell: We had inch and a half line, two and a half line, three-inch line. Four-inch line was unheard of at that time. There was no Smith valve yet. We had to come down to the Academy for the training on it. I was still in Five Engine so it had to be before '79.

130

As the new guy, it was my job to climb to the top of the hose-well and pull everything up. It was a hell of a climb. About three quarters of the way up, the ladder was shaky; the firehouse was kind of old. You wonder which day you're going to climb up and everything is going to fall down on you. If you looked down there was a pit about eight feet deep at the bottom of the well. That was always full almost to the top with water that never drained. I'm surprised so many firemen made it to retirement without picking up any diseases.

Langevin: If there were hose from the night before, you'd hang it because the jackets were cotton. Not like the synthetic fibers that we have today where we can roll them up wet and put them away, they needed to be drained and air dried. The ones that were in the tower that were dry were taken down and put back on the apparatus. The ones that were wet were hung in the tower. That's the first thing we did every morning. Usually the red-ass ended up climbing the ladder in the hose-well. I got to go up there several times.

Perdon: When I got to Six Engine we were still hanging hose. Two and a half, we were still hanging two and a half, three inch. That's where we dried it and it had to dry. We hadn't made that full change yet. I remember still in Six Engine going to the hose-well for more than sending it down to the hose shop.

Yes, we used it. Not long into being in Six Engine, but when I first got there. We didn't have two loads of hose, so it's a transitional period.

We had the fog nozzle. You know your combination. You had straight stream, but other than that it was pretty standard. They started giving us Task Master and little stuff like that, but pretty much it was just like today.

The only thing, we went to the pistol grip, but you bought them on your own at first. Guys would spend their own money to get the pistol grip. Then the city started buying them, but the nozzles were pretty much the same thing, fog, straight.

Gesualdo: Hose, we carried three inch hose for a hydrant feed, two and a half for our master stream and deck gun and inch and a half attack lines with Select-o-Matic two fifty, SM-250 nozzles, no pistol grips at the time. And it was a cotton jacket and then I vaguely remember hanging hose. I'm pretty sure that was mostly only three inch I think we used to hang. I seem to remember hanging three inch once in a while, but the rest of it we just collected back onto the apparatus.

Chapter Six: Ladders and Tools

Vesey: They bought two Pirsches during the war. The ground ladders on them were wooden. But anything new coming in was all metal ladders as I remember. The change was gradual. Anything new had to be according to the specs. I worked with wooden ladders. That forty-five wooden was a bitch. We didn't throw that up too often. The metal was a little lighter, but the forty-five still had the tormentors on them.

Masterson: After I made that rescue on Emmet Street, all the engines got thirty-five foot extension ladders. Engines, the only thing they had was twenty foot ladders. They were short. They were no good for the third floor. They wouldn't reach it right. I was just looking to make that grab, but then after that we all got thirty-five foot extension ladders on the engines, two sections. Because they couldn't put a big one on, they had to have two sections because the engines had no room to carry it.

Wall: Our ground ladders at the time were all wooden ladders. Even on the Pirsch they were all wooden. It was a Second World War thing and metal at that time was rationed. There was something to be said about the old wooden ladders. When they switched over to metal, a lot of us didn't like it. A lot of us felt that the metal ladders weren't as safe and secure. They were much narrower. A thirty-five or fifty foot was a hell of a lot narrower in metal than they were in wood. We felt more secure with the wooden ladders even though they were heavier. It took four guys to throw up a thirty-five foot ladder, but we actually trained where we could throw it up adequately with three guys, two guys who knew what they were doing and one guy footing it. We had the fifty-foot ladders with the bangers. That took six guys, but we could do that with four, a good truck company.

It was up to your captain on your tour whether you drilled or you didn't drill. Joe Zieser was a straight-line guy. You drilled with Zieser. In fact, he was of the old school mentally. If you went to a false alarm, you threw a twenty-four foot ladder up to mark the building. There was no fire. Throw a twenty-four up on that building. If there was a fire with an obvious life hazard or ventilation problem, you went immediately to your aerial. Other than that, with the older officers like Zieser, you'd throw a ground ladder. The whole idea there was if a firefighter were caught on the inside, they would know that there was a ladder in the front of the building. The second due truck was supposed to throw a similar ladder up in the rear. When you were inside, you knew you could go either front or back and you'd find a ground ladder to get out.

Freeman: You did ladder the building then. When there was a good fire, ladders went up. I don't know when they got away from that, but the buildings were always laddered. The ladders would go up in the front, at least one or two and if you could get into the side, sometimes they would ladder the side and possibly the back also. The trucks had the wooden truss ladders. You had to have the truss side a certain way. They were heavy. The engine carried a wooden roof ladder and I think it was a sixteen.

McGee: The trucks didn't have the steel Halligans hooks that we have now. They had wooden handled hooks with a sharp pointed edge. I think they were better. They would get right up and in there. The newer hooks have a wider brim on the top of them and sometimes they're not as penetrating as the old hooks were.

134

Stoffers: We had one metal ladder. It was a twenty-five foot extension and it was a dog. You had to clean and inspect the wooden ladders. The metal ladders were a little lighter, but when you used them they were both about the same, as long as the engine companies would leave room for the truck to get in. I always said, "You can put fifty foot more hose on those lines. You can't put five foot on a ladder."

Denvir: The ladders were all wood truss ladders that were heavy. They had a twenty-eight foot, twenty-four foot, and twenty-foot straight ground ladders. Then they had the thirty-five foot extension ladders.

Miller: We had all these wooden ladders that you had to take off all the time to wash, varnish, and make sure there were no splinters on them. Very cumbersome, very heavy, they needed at least three or four guys to raise the forty-five with extension at that time.

Butler: Equipment on the rigs, a lot of heavy equipment at that time. All the hooks were solid steel bars with the little hook head on top of them. Very heavy, very clumsy, awkward to work with, axes were the same as they are today. Saws, mechanical saws, were just about unheard of. You might have had one or two in the city, but maybe the Rescue Squad or Salvage companies the only ones that carried them. Any floors that had to be opened or roofs opened were all done by axe. No saws available at that time.

When I first entered the fire service, all ground ladders were wooden. As they come along, they started going to some steel ladders. They found out that steel wasn't the answer anyway because they actually turned out to be heavier than wooden ladders. Today you're seeing all aluminum ladders including most of the aerial ladders themselves. The city has all rear mount aerials now. No tillerman required and almost all the ladders are aluminum constructed. When I first came on every hook and ladder in the city was a tiller operated ladder.

Eleven Truck got a rear mount aerial device. The city had some money left over and gave it to the fire department. Deputy Chief Ed Wall was in charge of the Training Academy at that time. He went out shopping and came back with an aerial ladder that was sitting on an apparatus dealer's lot. The order had been cancelled by the town that had ordered it and they had already had it constructed and delivered to this dealer. The City of Newark virtually going out and shopping for something, picked it right off a lot.

Wargo: The wooden ladders were much heavier. I was a short, skinny guy when I came on the job. Some of the wooden ladders probably weighed as much as I did. So, it was pretty hard. You do learn and there are ways of getting around things. It worked out all right. Of course, they were changed. Before too long, they were going over to all the metal ladders. The wooden ladders made a lot of difference. They were heavy to put up, the big ones.

Prachar: Your tools are different. We didn't have K-12s in '68. You were lucky if you had a chain saw. Some companies like Five Truck, the busier truck companies, they had chain saws that they used on the roofs or you used the old axe. That's how I was taught.

McDonnell: I went from wood ladders to aluminum ladders. When I was at One Truck we had aluminum ladders. We had ground ladders that were wooden on other rigs. I went to Five Truck. They still had some wooden ladders. Used them and they were heavy as all hell. It was like a mix. I didn't work that much with the wooden ladders to have that good of an idea of the difference. The ladders during my middle time on the job were probably the best.

Now they're making more sections with a ground ladder because the rig was smaller. That big ladder, that two section thirty-five didn't fit on the rig a lot of times. The beds were so small. Those ladders, the three-section twenty-four foot ladder, were killers. So you needed more men. There were guys, they could raise the two section thirty-five by themselves. Ray Stoffers could do it. Richie Bennett could do it. Ronnie Ricca could do it. You could raise a thirty-five with two guys. But you start getting three-section ladders, they're murder. You need three guys to raise the main ladder. I never cared for that, putting that extra section on the ladder. It made it so heavy. A three- section thirty-five is a tough ladder to raise. You seem like you're pulling on that halyard forever.

T. Grehl: We had a forty-five, might have been a fifty, but I think it was forty-five foot ladder with the poles. We don't even have them on our rigs today. The only time I've ever seen one raised was when Joe Ricca worked overtime and decided he wanted to drill on a forty-five foot with the poles on a Saturday night at seven o'clock. That's the only time I think I've ever raised it other than at the Academy.

List of Interviewees

Baldino, Captain Barney, letter to the author 20 September, 2002. (appointed 1951)

Belzger, Firefighter William, 4 October, 2004, transcript. (appointed 1959)

Bisogna, Captain Joseph, 25 July, 2001, transcript. (appointed 1974)

Butler, Captain James, 3 September 1993, transcript. (appointed 1963)

Cahill, Firefighter Joseph, 25 June 1991, transcript. (appointed 1963)

Carragher, Deputy Chief William, November 1994, transcript. (appointed 1960)

Carter, Battalion Chief Harry, 12 June, 1991, transcript. (appointed 1973)

Charpentier, Firefighter Frederick, 22 August 1993, transcript. (appointed 1959)

Cody, Battalion Chief James, 26 October 1999, transcript. (appointed 1964)

Connell, Battalion Chief Anthony, 26 February, 1999, 24 November, 2003. (appointed 1974)

Cosby, Firefighter Joseph, 22 August, 1991, transcript. (appointed 1969)

Denvir, Captain John, 13 September 1993, transcript. (appointed 1959)

Deutch, Firefighter Charles, 14 November 1993, transcript. (appointed 1953)

Dunn, Deputy Chief Edward, 14 August 1991, 29 August 1997, transcript. (appointed 1959)

Finucan, Deputy Chief James, 7 August 1991, transcript. (appointed 1969)

Freda, Deputy Chief Alfred, 12, 25, 26 July 1991, transcript. (appointed 1959)

Fredette, Firefighter Reggie, 3 November, 1993, transcript. (appointed 1942)

Freeman, Captain Richard, 20, 21 August 1991, transcript. (appointed 1956)

Garrity, Battalion Chief Joseph, May 1992, transcript. (appointed 1964)

Gesualdo, Captain Al, 21 July, 2003, transcript. (appointed 1978)

Grehl, Deputy Chief Frederick, 7 August 1993, transcript. (appointed 1948)

Grehl, Captain Thomas, 29 May, 2002, transcript. (appointed 1971)

Griffith, Chief Fire Alarm Operator Robert, 3 July, 1991, transcript. (appointed 1953)

Haran, Captain Edward, 5 February 2001, transcript. (appointed 1961)

Harris, Captain William, 13 December 1999, transcript. (appointed 1961)

Highsmith, Firefighter Gerald, 2 June 1994, transcript. (appointed 1963)

Kinnear, Deputy Chief David, 28 September 1992, transcript. (appointed 1947)

Knight, Firefighter Gerald, 19 June 1991, transcript. (appointed 1964)

Langenbach, Deputy Chief James, 24 October, 2002, transcript. (appointed 1973)

Langevin, Firefighter Robert, 23 February, 1999, transcript. (appointed 1974)

Luxton, Captain Charles, 14 January, 1999, transcript. (appointed 1973)

Marcell, Firefighter Andrew, 23 September 1998, transcript. (appointed 1959)

Masters, Firefighter Anthony, 24 March, 2004, transcript. (appointed 1947)

Masterson, Captain Andrew, 6 April, 2005, transcript. (appointed 1949)

McCormack, Sr. Deputy Chief James, 14 June 1991, transcript. (appointed 1949)

McDonnell, Captain Thomas, 30 March, 1999, 16 April, 1999, transcript. (appointed 1970)

McGee, Captain Raymond, 26 October 2000, transcript. (appointed 1956)

McGovern, Battalion Chief Thomas, 8 June, 2001, transcript. (appointed 1968)

McGrory. Deputy Chief Albert, 31 August 1991, transcript. (appointed 1957)

Melodick, Firefighter William, June, 2001, transcript. (appointed 1970)

Miller, Battalion Chief Joseph, 16, 21 August 1991, transcript. (appointed 1959)

Perdon, Captain George, 9 June, 2003, transcript. (appointed 1974)

Pianka, Firefighter George, 15 June, 2001, transcript. (appointed 1970)

Pignato, Captain Nicholas, 26 May, 1999, transcript. (appointed 1974)

Prachar, Captain Daniel, 12 August, 1991, transcript. (appointed 1968)

Redden, Fire Chief Joseph, 16 September 2002, transcript. (appointed 1947)

Ricca, Battalion Chief Ronald, 1 June, 2000, transcript. (appointed 1974)

Rotonda, Firefighter Gerard, 3 May, 2000, transcript. (appointed 1970)

Ryan, Battalion Chief Joseph, 28 September, 1999, transcript. (appointed 1973)

Smith, Firefighter James, 2 September 1998, transcript. (appointed 1959)

Stoffers, Battalion Chief Carl, 2 September 1998, transcript. (appointed 1956)

Vesey, Firefighter Edward, 15 June 1999, transcript. (appointed 1948)

Vetrini, Captain Joseph, 14 September, 1993, transcript. (appointed 1946)

Wall, Deputy Chief Edward, 13 September, 2000, transcript. (appointed 1954)

Wargo, Captain Andrew, 6 June 1991, transcript. (appointed 1964)

www.ingramcontent.com/pod-product-compliance
Lightning Source LLC
LaVergne TN
LVHW011354080426
835511LV00005B/290